D0562847

Wigan

Liverpool

Chester

Shrewsbury

ENGLAND

Hereford

Bristol

Great Ormes
Head

Holyhead

Anglesey

Holy
Island

Bangor

Caernarfon

**ANGLESEY
& LLEYN
PENINSULA**

Lleyn Peninsula

Llandudno

Conwy

Rhyl

Denbigh

Mold

Wrexham

Betws-y-
Coed

**SNOWDONIA:
MOUNTAINS &
VALLEYS**

1085
Snowdon

Porthmadog

Bala

Llangollen

**NORTHEAST
WALES &
MARCHES**

Dolgellau

Welshpool

Barmouth

CARDIGAN
BAY

Machynlleth

Aberystwyth

Llangurig

Rhayader

Knighton

**BRECON BEACONS
& MID WALES**

Aberaeron

Llandrindod
Wells

Strumble
Head

Fishguard

Cardigan

Lampeter

Hay-on-Wye

St David's

PEMBROKESHIRE

Haverfordwest

Carmarthen

Llandovery

Brecon

Abergavenny

Monmouth

Pembroke

Llanelli

Llandeilo

Brecon Beacons

Merthyr
Tydfil

Cwmbran

Chepstow

Swansea

Gower

Neath

**GOWER PENINSULA
& COAST**

Newport

Caerphilly

Bridgend

Cardiff

Bristol

BRISTOL CHANNEL

Lundy

6 Walk start point

1 Cycle start point

3 Tour start point

LINDENHURST MEMORIAL LIBRARY
One Lee Avenue
Lindenhurst, New York 11757

Wales

Author: John Gillham
Verifier: Neil Coates
Managing Editor: David Popey
Project Management: Bookwork Creative Associates Ltd
Designers: Liz Baldin of Bookwork and Andrew Milne
Picture Library Manager: Ian Little
Picture Research: Vivien Little and Alice Earle
Cartography provided by the Mapping Services Department of AA Publishing
Copy-editors: Marilynne Lanng of Bookwork and Pamela Stagg
Internal Repro and Image Manipulation: Jacqueline Street
Production: Rachel Davis

Produced by AA Publishing
© AA Media Limited 2007
Reprinted 2007, 2008, 2009
Updated and revised 2010

All rights reserved. No part of this publication may be reproduced, stored in a retrieval system in any
form or by any means – electronic, photocopying, recording or otherwise – unless the written
permission of the publishers has been obtained beforehand.

Published by AA Publishing (a trading name of AA Media Limited, whose registered office is Fanum
House, Basing View, Basingstoke, Hampshire RG21 4EA; registered number 06112600).

 This product includes mapping data licensed from the Ordnance Survey®
with the permission of the Controller of Her Majesty's Stationery Office.
© Crown Copyright 2011. All rights reserved. Licence number 100021153.

ISBN 978-0-7495-6695-1 (T)
ISBN 978-0-7495-6708-8 (SS)

A CIP catalogue record for this book is available from the British Library.

The contents of this book are believed correct at the time of printing. Nevertheless, the publishers
cannot be held responsible for any errors or omissions or for changes in the details given in this
book or for the consequences of any reliance on the information it provides. This does not affect your
statutory rights. We have tried to ensure accuracy in this book, but things do change and we would be
grateful if readers would advise us of any inaccuracies they may encounter.

We have taken all reasonable steps to ensure that the walks and cycle rides in this book are safe and
achievable by people with a realistic level of fitness. However, all outdoor activities involve a degree of
risk and the publishers accept no responsibility for any injuries caused to readers while following
these walks and cycle rides. For advice on walking and cycling in safety, see pages 16–17.

Some of the walks and cycle routes may appear in other AA books.

Visit AA Publishing at theAA.com/shop

Printed and bound in China by C&C

A04393

CONTENTS

Welcome to...
Wales

There's something special about crossing the borders into Wales. Maybe it is the way the flat fields of the English shires soar up into the Welsh hills, or those funny sounding, unpronounceable place names on the road signs. When I see the 'Croeso i Gymru' – Welcome to Wales – sign, my spirits lift, my pulse quickens and those mountains call.

Borderland Wales is fertile and verdant, with rolling foothills rising to high, heather moors. Pretty villages set deep into little-known valleys like the Ceiriog and the Tanat south of Llangollen just wait to be discovered.

The Conwy Valley marks the transition to the mountainous heartlands of Wales: Snowdonia. Here the great Carneddau whalebacks decline to the sea, backed up by the distinctive craggy Glyderau range and Snowdon itself. All 15 of the 3,000-foot (915m) Welsh peaks lie in a compact region between Conwy, Caernarfon and Beddgelert. Villages at the foot of the mountains like Capel Curig, Betws-y-Coed and Llanberis are dedicated to walkers and climbers. But for those who don't climb, you're never far from the yawning sands of the coast, one of those wonderful narrow-gauge steam railways or one of the great 13th-century castles built by Edward I as part of his 'iron ring' to repress the Welsh warrior princes.

In absolute contrast to Snowdonia's alpine scenery, the moorland peaks and cwms of the Elenydd region of Mid Wales are simpler in form, with wild and remote upland plateaux opening out to big, big skies.

The great flat-topped sandstone escarpments of the Brecon Beacons mark the entry to South Wales, where rural landscapes descend deep into 'the valleys'. From the Industrial Revolution onwards, the valleys were the engine room of Wales. Coal, iron and steel fuelled an economy that led to massive growth in the ports of Cardiff, Swansea and Newport. After years the decline of these industries posed challenges but, remembering their maritime roots, the towns and cities have been revitalised. Cardiff's vibrant new bay area with its barrage, marinas, Millennium Centre and Senedd Building brings thousands of visitors every week.

Wales meets the Atlantic Ocean at Pembrokeshire, whose spectacular coast is as rugged as anything Cornwall can offer. Unlike the West Country, Pembrokeshire can offer the coast without the crowds, and quaint fishing villages without those huge coach parks.

Wigan

Liverpool

Chester

Shrewsbury

ENGLAND

Hereford

Bristol

ANGLESEY & LLEYN PENINSULA

SNOWDONIA: MOUNTAINS & VALLEYS

NORTHEAST WALES & MARCHES

BRECON BEACONS & MID WALES

PEMBROKESHIRE

GOWER PENINSULA & COAST

CARDIGAN BAY

BRISTOL CHANNEL

Great Ormes Head

Holyhead
Holy Island
Anglesey
Caernarfon
Bangor
Conwy
Llandudno
Rhyl
Denbigh
Mold
Wrexham
1085 Snowdon
Betws-y-Coed
Llangollen
Porthmadog
Bala
Lleyn Peninsula
Dolgellau
Barmouth
Welshpool
Machynlleth
Aberystwyth
Llangurig
Rhayader
Knighton
Aberaeron
Llandrindod Wells
Strumble Head
Cardigan
Lampeter
Hay-on-Wye
Fishguard
St David's
Haverfordwest
Carmarthen
Llandovery
Brecon
Abergavenny
Monmouth
Pembroke
Llandeilo
Merthyr Tydfil
Cwmbran
Chepstow
Llanelli
Gower
Swansea
Neath
Newport
Caerphilly
Bridgend
Cardiff
Lundy

Cambrian Mountains

Brecon Beacons

6	Walk start point
1	Cycle start point
3	Tour start point

ESSENTIAL SIGHTS

Visit Cardiff Castle and enjoy a wealth of culture and good shopping...gaze across the Brecon Beacons...get up very high in the Snowdonia National Park...walk along the coast at Pembrokeshire or enjoy the views on the spectacular Gower Peninsula...explore the vast expanse of Fforest Fawr and the Black Mountain... discover waterfall country...visit Edward I's castles at Carnaerfon, Conwy or Laugharne...visit Machynlleth for an alternative view on modern living...take a ride on the Brecon Mountain Railway...visit the charming border town of Chepstow or walk part of Offa's Dyke...admire Thomas Telford's feat of bridge engineering across the Menai Strait or the Victorian dam of Craig Goch Reservoir, which holds back the waters of the Elan Valley...discover the mysteries of Preseli and St David's or the delightful harbour at Milford Haven.

1 Offa's Dyke
This important boundary ditch and embankment was built in the 8th century by the Mercian king Offa to divide England and Wales. It runs from Prestatyn in the north to Sedbury near Chepstow in the south.

2 Criccieth Castle
Built around 1230 for Llywelyn the Great, this superb castle stands on a headland above the lovely seaside town of Criccieth.

3 Bala
Steam engines, which once worked in the slate quarries of North Wales, are now put to use hauling passenger coaches from Llanuwchyllyn station along the lakeside to Bala.

4 Portmeirion
Welsh architect Sir Clough Williams-Ellis built this fairytale Italianate village on a peninsula on the shores of Cardigan Bay.

5 Snowdonia
The National Park is a great place for climbing and walking with routes of varying difficulties, from gentle strolls in the valleys to more demanding routes on the mountain tops. Make sure you're properly equipped for your chosen routes or activities.

6 Menai Strait
Thomas Telford's fine suspension bridge of 1826 strides gracefully across the Menai Strait, linking ancient Anglesey with the Welsh mainland.

7 Conwy Castle
The imposing entrance to Edward I's superb 13th-century castle, which dominates the town of Conwy. The castle forms part of the town's original system of defence, which includes the town walls.

8 Brecon Beacons
The Brecon Beacons National Park, situated in Mid Wales, is a diverse landscape of open hills, mountains and lakes, and lowland areas of rolling farmland and woods.

9 Snowdon Horseshoe
One of the most popular circuits to the top of Mount Snowdon is the Horseshoe, which takes in the peaks of Crib Goch, Crib y Ddysgl, Yr Wydffa (Snowdon) and Liwedd.

10 Cardiff
The city's revamped Cardiff Bay waterfront area offers plenty of shops, bars, restaurants and visitor attractions, including the Wales Millennium Centre, a showpiece arts centre for Welsh culture.

6

7

8

9

10

Day One

For many people a weekend break or a long weekend is a popular way of spending their leisure time. These four pages offer a loosely planned itinerary designed to ensure that you make the most of your time, whatever the weather, and see and enjoy the very best of Wales.

The first day seeks out Monmouthshire's medieval history, visiting an abbey, four castles and an ancient gated bridge. It illustrates perfectly the beauty of Wales' southern border county.

Friday Night

Make your way to the border town of Chepstow. If there's time, take a walk around its pretty streets and ginnels to see the 13th-century town walls and the imposing Norman castle, which is set high on cliffs overlooking the River Wye. The Castle View Inn is the perfect choice for a relaxing start to the weekend, with fine food and accommodation.

Saturday Morning

It's well worth taking a closer look at Chepstow Castle. Now run by CADW, the castle's construction in stone began in the same year as the Battle of Hastings. The A466 to the west of the town takes the route through the beautiful Wye Valley. Visit the 12th-century Cistercian abbey at Tintern. Though roofless, the abbey is still one of the most elegant ecclesiastical buildings in Wales.

Saturday Lunch

Take a leisurely lunch at the Tintern Abbey Hotel, where you can relax in the front garden, which overlooks the abbey and the River Wye.

Saturday Afternoon

The Wye meets the Monnow at historic Monmouth, birthplace of King Henry V and Charles Rolls of Rolls-Royce fame – their statues are in Agincourt Square. Don't miss the 13th-century Monnow Bridge, the only one in Britain to have a fortified gatehouse.

Follow lanes out of town to Skenfrith, which lies among green rolling hills several miles to the northwest. The castle (free entry) is idyllically set on a green by the banks of the Monnow – wonderful for picnics. More lanes lead westwards to White Castle, a fine moated 12th-century fortress.

Now head for Llanfihangel Crucorney, before following narrow lanes that wind through the stunningly beautiful Vale of Ewyas, which cuts through the Black Mountains. Half way along is Llanthony Priory (free entry), which surprisingly has it's own pub beneath the arches.

Saturday Night

The Gospel Pass at the head of the Vale of Ewyas has superb long distance views and is an ideal place to stop and stretch your legs. Descend to the literary town of Hay-on-Wye, where Kilverts offers good, comfortable accommodation and tasty meals in the bar or restaurant.

HAY-ON-WYE

LLANTHONY PRIORY

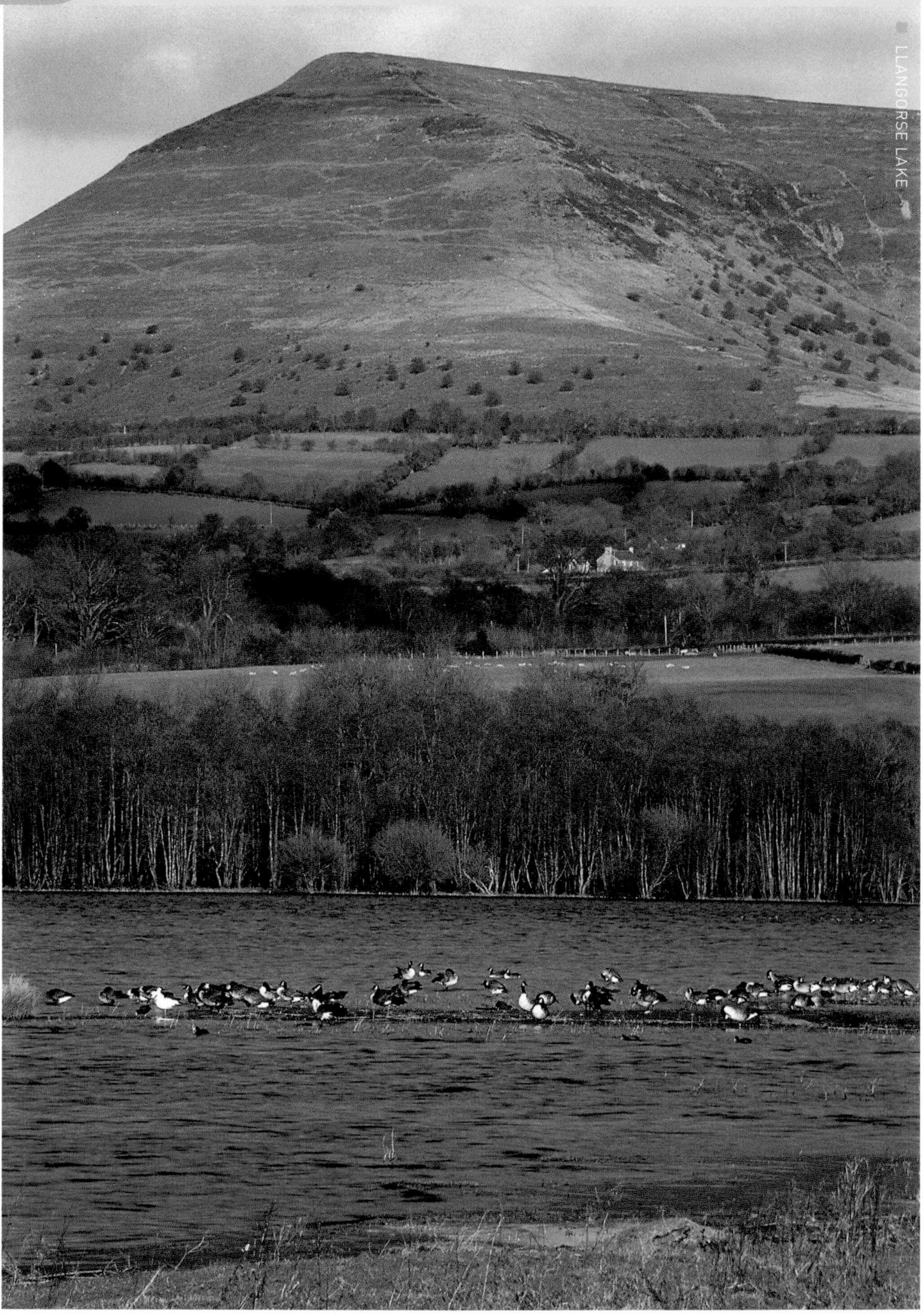

LLANGORSE LAKE

Day Two

Our second and final day offers the chance to explore the Brecon Beacons National Park. After a relaxing start, the day gets going with a drive to Llangorse for lunch and a visit to the lake. In the afternoon there's an opportunity for a walk on a clearly defined path or you can take a ride on the Brecon Mountain Railway, one of Wales' great little steam railways.

Sunday Morning

Hay-on-Wye is a fascinating little market town. On Sunday morning, you'll find the town ticks over at a more leisurely pace. If the weather is fine and dry there is an easy and picturesque stroll by the river, which follows the Wye Valley Walk route westwards along the north bank. Many of the town's antiquarian bookshops open around mid-morning.

Head southwest out of the town, passing through Talgarth before taking the B4560 to Llangorse, a small village sheltering in the verdant lake-filled basin that is squeezed between the Black Mountains and the Brecon Beacons.

Sunday Lunch

Take lunch at the Red Lion at Llangorse and if there's time drive down to the lake, which has a lovely view across to the Beacons and is good for bird-watching.

Sunday Afternoon

After heading south to the A40, head for Talybont-on-Usk, where quiet country lanes track alongside the lovely Talybont Reservoir and up to a high pass to the south of the main Brecon Beacons ridge. If it's fine and you have some walking boots, a map and three hours to spare, the clearly defined there-and-back path is well worth doing.

The lane descends into the afforested valley of the Taf Fechan, past the Pentwyn Reservoir into Pontsticill village, where a right turn leads to Pant Station on the Brecon Mountain Railway. If you didn't do the walk, there should be plenty of time for a return trip on the narrow-gauge steam railway (it takes just over an hour). There's a licensed restaurant and children's play area by the station, so this is a good spot for supper before returning home.

Route facts

MINIMUM TIME The time stated for completing each route is the estimated minimum time that a reasonably fit family group of walkers or cyclists would take to complete the circuit. This does not allow for rest or refreshment stops.

OS MAP Each route is shown on a map. However, some detail is lost because of the restrictions imposed by scale, so for this reason, we recommend that you use the maps in conjunction with a more detailed Ordnance Survey map. The relevant map for each walk or cycle ride is listed.

START This indicates the start location and parking area. This is a six-figure grid reference prefixed by two letters showing which 62.5-mile (100km) square of the National Grid it refers to. You'll find more information on grid references on most Ordnance Survey maps.

CYCLE HIRE We list, within reason, the nearest cycle hire shop/centre.

❶ Here we highlight any potential difficulties or dangers along the cycle ride or walk. If a particular route is suitable for older, fitter children we say so here. Also, we give guidelines of a route's suitability for younger children, for example the symbol 8+ indicates that the route can probably be attempted by children aged 8 years and above.

Walks & Cycle Rides

Each walk and cycle ride has a panel giving information for the walker and cyclist, including the distance, terrain, nature of the paths, and where to park your car.

WALKING

All of the walks are suitable for families, but less experienced family groups, especially those with younger children, should try the shorter walks. Route finding is usually straightforward, but the maps are for guidance only and we recommend that you always take the relevant Ordnance Survey map with you.

Risks

Although each walk has been researched with a view to minimising any risks, no walk in the countryside can be considered to be completely free from risk. Walking in the outdoors will always require a degree of common sense and judgement to ensure that it is as safe as possible, especially for young children.

• Be particularly careful on cliff paths and in upland terrain, where the consequences of a slip can be serious.

• Remember to check tidal conditions before walking on the seashore.

• Some sections of route are by, or cross, busy roads.

Remember traffic is a danger even on minor country lanes.

• Be careful around farmyard machinery and livestock.

• Be prepared for the consequences of changes in the weather and check the forecast before you set out.

• Ensure the whole family is properly equipped, wearing suitable clothing and a good pair of boots or sturdy walking shoes. Take waterproof clothing with you and a torch if you are walking in the winter months.

• Remember the weather can change quickly at any time of the year, and in moorland and heathland areas, mist and fog can make route-finding much harder. In summer, take account of the heat and sun by wearing a hat, sunscreen and carrying enough water.

• On walks away from centres of population you should carry a mobile phone, whistle and, if possible, a survival bag. If you do have an accident requiring emergency services, make a note of your position as accurately as possible and dial 999 (112 on a mobile).

CYCLING

In devising the cycle rides in this guide, every effort has been made to use designated cycle paths, or to link them with quiet country lanes and waymarked byways and bridleways. In a few cases, some fairly busy B-roads have been used to join up with quieter routes.

Rules of the road

• Ride in single file on narrow and busy roads.

• Be alert, look and listen for traffic, especially on narrow lanes and blind bends and be extra careful when descending steep hills, as loose gravel or a poor road surface can lead to an accident.

• In wet weather make sure that you keep an appropriate distance between you and other riders.

• Make sure you indicate your intentions clearly.

• Brush up on *The Highway Code* before venturing out onto the road.

Off-road safety code of conduct

• Only ride where you know it is legal to do so. Cyclists are not allowed to cycle on public footpaths (yellow waymarks). The only 'rights of way' open to cyclists are bridleways (blue markers) and unsurfaced tracks, known as byways, which are open to all traffic and waymarked in red.

• Canal tow paths: you need a permit to cycle on some stretches of tow path (www. waterscape.com). Remember that access paths can be steep and slippery so always push your bike under low bridges and by locks.

• Always yield to walkers and horses, giving adequate warning of your approach.

• Don't expect to cycle at high speeds.

• Keep to the main trail to avoid any unnecessary erosion to the area beside the trail and to prevent skidding, especially in wet weather conditions.

• Remember to follow the Country Code

Preparing your bicycle

Check the wheels, tyres, brakes and cables. Lubricate hubs, pedals, gear mechanisms and cables. Make sure you have a pump, a bell, a rear rack to carry panniers and a set of lights.

Equipment

• A cycling helmet provides essential protection.

• Make sure you are visible to other road users, by wearing light-coloured or luminous clothing in daylight and sashes or reflective strips in failing light and darkness.

• Take extra clothes with you, depending on the season, and a wind/waterproof jacket.

• Carry a basic tool kit, a pump, a strong lock and a first aid kit.

• Always carry enough water for your outing.

Walk Map Legend

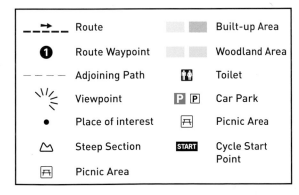

--→--	Route		Built-up Area
❶	Route Waypoint		Woodland Area
- - - -	Adjoining Path	👫	Toilet
☀	Viewpoint	P P	Car Park
•	Place of interest	🏠	Picnic Area
⌒	Steep Section	**START**	Cycle Start Point
🏠	Picnic Area		

NEFYN

Anglesey & Lleyn Peninsula

The Menai Strait, between the castle-crowned towns of Beaumaris and Caernarfon, has always set Anglesey apart from its Welsh neighbours. Its dolmen-dotted interior is fringed by a coastline of steep cliffs and sandy bays. Over on the mainland, the narrow coastal plains rear up to the cloud-capped foothills of Snowdonia. Separated by a mere sliver of water, it's not surprising that Anglesey and the Lleyn Peninsula have much in common.

1 Walk start point

MOELFRE

CAERNARFON CASTLE

Unmissable attractions

Visit Aberdaron, picture-postcard pretty and filled with whitewashed cottages, and a wide sand and pebble beach popular with watersports enthusiasts...take a walk along the coast and spot the colonies of sea birds at South Stack...gaze across the moat to Beaumaris Castle, perhaps the most beautiful of Edward I's castles, built in the late 13th century or Caernarfon, the most ambitious, intended to be the seat of government and the monarch's official residence...explore the wildlife habitat at Newborough Warren, a National Nature Reserve, which covers 1,500 acres (607ha) of shifting sand dunes and forest plantations...enjoy the hydrangeas that blossom in the mild climate at Plas Newydd, on the banks of the Menai Strait.

1

1 **South Stack Lighthouse**
Located near Holyhead on Anglesey, South Stack Lighthouse Visitor Centre is reached via a flight of steps to a suspension bridge to the island.

2 **Beaumaris**
One of King Edward's most complete and romantic-looking castles, Beaumaris was built to guard the approach to the Menai Strait and Anglesey.

3 **Pwllheli**
The hills of the Lleyn Peninsula rise beyond Pwllheli's elegant promenade and beach.

4 **Caernarfon Castle**
Imposing and stately, Caernarfon Castle is the most impressive of King Edward I's fortifications.

ABERDARON & BARDSEY ISLAND MAP REFS SH1726 & SH1121

Aberdaron is often described in tourist leaflets as being the Land's End of North Wales. This is being more than kind to the, in my opinion, over-commercialised Land's End and unkind to Aberdaron, for this old fishing village, which lies at the mouth of the River Daron and at the end of the Lleyn Peninsula, is chocolate-box pretty, with lovely whitewashed cottages gleaming against a backdrop of blue sea and golden cliffs and is steeped in the history of Celtic saints and pilgrims. Old Y Gegin Fawr café, in the centre of the village by the little stone bridge, dates from the 13th century, when it was used as a communal kitchen for the pilgrims on their way to Bardsey Island.

Aberdaron's wide sand and pebble beach is popular for fishing, watersports and bathing. From here, pick up the Lleyn Coastal Path for a fabulous walk to Pen y Cil Point and views to Bardsey.

■ Visit

NEWBOROUGH WARREN AND FOREST

Newborough Warren was created in the 13th century when storms buried farmland beneath sand dunes. Rabbits were soon to colonise the area, hence its name. To save the village of Newborough from further sand encroachment, Queen Elizabeth I made it an offence to cut down the dunes' natural vegetation, marram grass, which was used for mat-making. Later on, a pine forest was planted to offer further protection. Now a national nature reserve, the dunes and slacks of the area host many species of wild flowers including the marsh orchid and grass of Parnassus; there are red squirrels, too.

St Hywyn's Church, which is located right next to the beach, is in two halves, one dating back to 1137 and the other, an extension, around 1400. The poet R S Thomas (1913–2000), a nominee for the Nobel Prize for Literature, was the local vicar here between 1954 and 1967 and the church contains interpretations of his life and works. The exposed position of the church has resulted in damage from sea's proximity over the years, but it is now being restored to the glory days when it would have been the last stop for those many intrepid pilgrims, before they ventured across the wild – and sometimes – treacherous waters to Bardsey Island (Ynys Enlli).

Modern day travellers can take a boat trip to Bardsey from Porth Meudwy, around the bay from Aberdaron. Visitors often get to see dolphins, porpoises and seals on their way across. They'll surely spot at least some of the island's 16,000 breeding pairs of Manx shearwaters. Bardsey, which is just over 2 miles (3km) long and rises to 548 feet (167m) at Mynydd Enlli, has been designated a National Nature Reserve. Celtic monks settled here in the 6th century but only the tower remains of the 13th-century, Augustinian abbey. Many graves have been discovered on the island, giving rise to the claim that it is the resting place of 20,000 saints.

BEAUMARIS MAP REF SH6076

These days the busy, non-stop A55 dual carriageway speeds most tourists on their way to Holyhead for the ferryboat crossings to both Dublin and Dun Laoghaire in Ireland. Telford's graceful

◼ Visit

THE WELSH HIGHLAND RAILWAY

Originally completed as a slate railway linking Caernarfon and Porthmadog, this ambitious line lasted only 18 years before closure in 1941. Following years of dedicated work, the line fully reopened in 2010, offering the prospect of a mouth-watering journey through the beautiful, mountainous countryside around the skirts of Snowdon to pretty Beddgelert and through the spectacular Aberglaslyn Pass. At Porthmadog it links with the Ffestiniog Railway, creating one of Europe's most extensive narrow-gauge railway systems.

◼ Visit

CAERNARFON AIRWORLD AVIATION MUSEUM

Perhaps the perfect museum for anyone interested in flight, the Aviation Museum based at Caernarfon Airport, Dinas Dinlle, tells the story of the RAF and the Mountain Rescue Service. It has plenty of combat aircraft, including the Hawker Hunter, the Vampire and Javelin, and you can even sit inside some of the cockpits. You can watch aviation footage in the small cinema and there is a museum gift shop.

◼ Visit

DIN LLIGWY – AN ANCIENT VILLAGE

Hidden in woodland, a mile (1.6km) or so inland from Moelfre, is a wonderfully preserved Celtic settlement. The half-acre (0.2ha) site consists of foundations of a number of buildings, with the entire area enclosed by a thick double wall, which would have been built in the 4th century AD, during the last years of the Roman Empire. In a nearby field are the remains of a neolithic burial chamber, the Lligwy tomb. A massive capstone weighing about 25 tons covers the remains of 15 to 30 people, and pieces of beaker and grooved ware pottery were also discovered.

suspension bridge of 1824 now carries local traffic, but it is still a superb sight, enhanced by the dramatic backdrop of the peaks of Snowdonia's mountains. After the busy village of Menai Bridge you'll find the small town of Beaumaris, which is dominated by its 13th-century castle. Edward I chose the site, which he said should be called beau marais, which means fair marsh. Beaumaris Castle is regarded as one of the finest examples of Master James of St George's designs and wasn't finished due to lack of money and supplies. Although the walls never reached their intended height, the low-slung look is quite appealing and with the filled moat, four concentric layers of fortifications, private sea dock and surrounding parkland, it's most people's idea of a perfect castle. Beaumaris town dates largely from the Victorian period, although the courthouse opposite the castle dates back to 1614. It is a major yachting centre – the Royal Anglesey Yacht Club resides here – and regular boat trips, for fishing or sightseeing, start from the pier.

CAERNARFON MAP REF SH4862

Dominated by its majestic 13-towered castle, Caernarfon guards the mouth of the Afon Seiont (Saint River) and the western end of the Menai Strait.

The castle is the most imposing of Edward I's 'iron ring'. Begun in 1283 on the site of a motte and bailey castle, it would become a royal palace, designed to symbolise domination over the Welsh. It's an impressive sight with its mighty polygonal towers and powerful ramparts that are remarkably intact. It is not surprising therefore that it was chosen by the Royal Family to be the setting for Prince Charles' investiture as Prince of Wales – some 700 years after Edward's son became the first English Prince of Wales in the same place. Caernarfon castle, now under the care of CADW, also houses the regimental Museum of the Royal Welch Fusiliers.

Powerful-looking medieval walls with imposing towered gates extend from the castle around the old town. The narrow streets are lined with many fascinating buildings. Some of these are Georgian and Victorian, but a few, including St Mary's Church, which is built into those walls, are much older. There is an informative town trail leaflet, available from the tourist information centre, which will guide you from the Castle Square through the old gates, around the old red light district of Northgate, where you'll see the 15th-century Black Boy Inn, the castle and the old Slate Quay. The trail illustrates that this was very much a seafaring town and the Maritime Museum on Bank Quay near Victoria Dock reinforces this, with a history of seafaring and industry in the area. Exhibits include models of ships, photographs and artefacts.

Caernarfon's long history predates the Normans by many centuries. The Romans, under the governance of Cnaeus Julius Agricola, conquered the Ordovices (an early Welsh tribe) in AD 77 and shortly afterwards established a fort, named, Segontium to the southeast of the present town. Like many Roman forts, Segontium had defences of earth and timber, with gates and parallel streets. At the height of its strength it would have housed a thousand troops, all non-Roman citizens called cohorts. One such regiment known to have served here was called the First Cohort of Sunici, recruited from Germany. Coins discovered at archaeological digs show that the Romans occupied Segontium until about AD 394, a very long span, which indicates its strategic importance. A very fine museum here exhibits and interprets artefacts from the Roman era.

HOLY ISLAND MAP REF SH2481

While Holyhead is the largest of all of Anglesey's towns, with a good yachting marina, a maritime museum, a beach (Penrhos) and the island's highest hill, it's a rather unattractive place, little more than a busy transit port for Ireland since the Act of Union 1801. A far better base to discover Holy Island would be Trearddur Bay on the wild southwest coast. St Brigit is said to have landed here at the end of the 5th century and the little church is dedicated to her. Here the coastline is heavily indented with rocky promontories, low cliffs and islets enclosing small sandy beaches. In the central region there is one superb sweeping sandy cove overlooked by a yacht club, the lifeboat station and the huge whitewashed Trearddur Bay Hotel, which is at the centre of all things local.

To the north of Trearddur the rough and rugged coastline becomes truly spectacular. The view from Ellins Tower, the RSPB information centre, to South Stack lighthouse is stunning. The cliffs of South Stack are a haven for flocks of seabirds including guillemots, skuas and gannets and the rare chough. When the wild west wind blows it's easy to see why Anglesey's perilous waters were the cause of so many terrible shipwrecks.

The limestone headland of Holyhead Mountain, which lies just beyond South Stack, looks much higher than its mere 719 foot (220m) altitude would imply. Clad with heathland it is capped by a huge Celtic fort, Cae'r y Twr, which was built on the site of a Roman watchtower.

MOELFRE & ANGLESEY'S COAST MAP REF SH5186

More than any other village in Anglesey, Moelfre has a history of dramatic and daring lifeboat rescues. You can find out all about them at the Moelfre Seawatch Centre, which is sited not far from the harbour. Whitewashed fishermen's cottages are scattered on the headland overlooking a small harbour, a shingle beach and the little island, Ynys Moelfre. There are wonderful clifftop paths to Dulas Bay, and in the opposite direction to Benllech and Red Wharf Bay.

Benllech is a modern-looking resort with a sandy beach and good facilities for families and visitors. Just a short walk southwards on the coastal path brings you to Red Wharf Bay where there's a huge expanse of sand, tidal mud and salt marshes – the fine sands stretch for 2.5 miles (4km) to Llandonna. The bay is absolutely superb for walking and birding: you'll more than likely spot redshanks, curlews, shelduck and oystercatchers. Anglesey's best pub, The Ship Inn, and the best restaurant, the Old Boat House, are here.

NEFYN & LLEYN'S COAST
MAP REF SH3040

Nefyn, the largest of Lleyn's northern coastal villages, has two long sandy beaches. The one below the main village is beautifully situated, sheltered by vegetated shaly cliffs and has stunning views back along the gently arcing bay to the mountains known as the Yr Eifl, (the Rivals). The view is slightly marred by a row of tatty sheds parading as beach huts. Porthdinllaen, the next cove beneath Morfa Nefyn, has the same shaly cliffs and a wonderful crescent-shaped sandy beach framed by a rocky promontory with an Iron Age fort on top. The Ty Coch pub here at Porthdinllaen has to be one of the best-sited pubs in Wales – it's right on the beach!

East of Nefyn the road turns inland to climb over the shoulders of Yr Eifl. Perched on the east summit of these granite mountains is Tre'r Ceiri, the 'town of giants' in legend but in reality one of the best-preserved ancient forts in Wales. A gigantic Bronze Age burial cairn lies in the centre of an elaborate ancient settlement, where shattered stone walls enclose dozens of well-formed hut circle foundations. It's well worth taking the zig-zag roadside path through the heather to see them. Lleyn's north coast gets more sparsely populated as you go westwards. This was largely the preserve of fishermen in days gone by – the locals still fish for crabs and lobsters – but the lonely cliffs, coves and beaches are a real haven for holiday-makers looking for a little elbow room. Porth Iago has a tiny rock-bound beach – on a sunny day here you could be forgiven for thinking you were in Sardinia or on one of the Greek Islands. Porth Oer, better known as Whistling Sands because the texture of the sand grains make them whistle underfoot, is a larger beach, backed by steep grassy cliffs, with safe bathing and a café.

PORTHMADOG & SOUTH LLEYN MAP REF SH5638

Centred around a small harbour and the causeway William Madocks built to reclaim land on the Glaslyn Estuary, Porthmadog is the most popular holiday resort in Lleyn. Many of the visitors come to take a train ride on one of the two narrow-gauge railways, the Welsh Highland, which trundles through to Caernarfon, and the Ffestiniog, which takes a scenic route to the lovely slate town of Blaenau Ffestiniog. A short walk leads past Porthmadog's boatyards and over a heavily wooded headland to reach the sheltered and picturesque beach at Borth y Guest, a village, where life is taken at a leisurely pace.

A few miles further west lies Criccieth, whose castle stands on a huge rhyolite crag that juts out into Tremadog Bay. It's part of Edward I's 'iron ring' but, as there was already a Welsh castle on the spot, the English king only had to annexe and enlarge it. The twin-towered gatehouse was built by Llywelyn the Great in around 1240. The castle was left in its current ruinous state in 1404 after being captured by Welsh prince Owain Glyndwr. Despite its one-time strategic importance, Criccieth remained a small fishing port until the Victorians' craving for sun and sand saw it grow to today's

proportions. There are two sand and shingle beaches either side of the castle and some excellent restaurants, cafés and bistros. Nearby Llanystumdwy was the boyhood home of one-time British Prime Minister David Lloyd George.

Pwllheli, often considered to be the capital of Lleyn, has plenty of facilities, including a magnificent marina, and is considered an international yachting centre. Although the town is good for shopping, it has a rather charmless urban sprawl, and there are better beaches elsewhere.

Abersoch is a lively resort whose fine sandy beach and dunes are sheltered from the wild Atlantic winds by the Cilan headland, the eastern jaw of Hell's Mouth. The shelter has helped Abersoch grow into an international centre for yachting: there is some sort of regatta or race almost every summer weekend. The village itself is ringed around a large harbour. Abersoch also caters for windsurfing, water-skiing, wakeboarding and bodyboarding.

■ Visit

PORTMEIRION

In 1925, the Welsh architect Sir Clough Williams-Ellis began building Portmeirion in the elegant style of an Italian village, on a peninsula off the Tremadog Bay coast. His intention was to illustrate how 'the development of a naturally beautiful site need not lead to its defilement'. Gorgeous pastel-coloured buildings in the small town blend perfectly with the 60-acre (24ha) subtropical gardens splashed with the colours of azaleas, rhododendrons and hydrangeas. The privately owned village (entry free) found fame in th 1960s TV series *The Prisoner*.

Around Holyhead Mountain

This is the last stop before Ireland, and rugged and rocky Holy Island offers some of the best walking in Anglesey. The path from the car park heads straight for a white castellated building known as Ellins Tower. This former summerhouse is now an RSPB seabird centre. The surrounding area will fascinate birders as it is a breeding ground for puffins, razorbills, guillemots and the rare maritime chough: a closed-circuit video camera shows live pictures.The footpath traverses splendid maritime heath dominated by heather, bell heather and stunted western gorse.

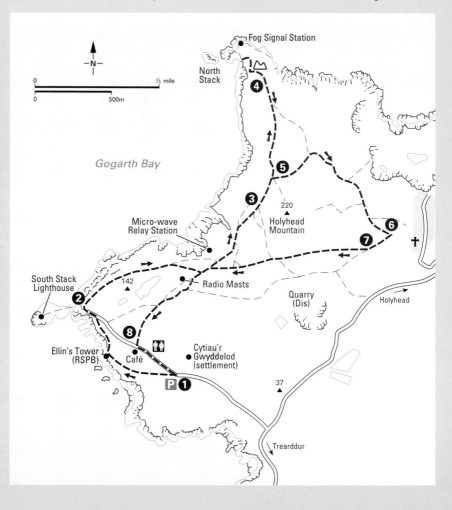

Route Directions

1 Take the path for the RSPB centre at Ellin's Tower, a small white castellated building, then climb along the path back to the road which should be followed along to its end.

2 If you're not visiting the South Stack Lighthouse, climb right on a path passing a stone shelter. The path detours right to round the BT aerials and dishes. At a crossroads go left, heading back to the coast, then take the left fork. Ignore the next left, a dead end path and continue following waymarks over the north shoulder of Holyhead Mountain.

3 Ignore paths leading off right to the summit, but keep left on a good path heading north towards North Stack.

4 After passing through a grassy walled enclosure the path descends in zig-zags down steep slopes. Joining a track follow it left to a rocky platform, where the Fog Signal Station and the island of North Stack come into full view. Retrace your steps back up the zig-zags and towards Holyhead Mountain.

5 At a junction below the summit path, turn sharp left across the heath. Go right at its end, contouring the eastern side of the mountain. Keep right at a fork and then ignore another summit path from the right. Beyond the mountain, take a right fork as the path comes to a wall. Follow the path downhill towards rough pastureland.

6 Go down a grassy walled track before turning right along another, similar one. This soon becomes a rough path traversing more heathland, now to the south of Holyhead Mountain.

7 Where a waymarked path is later signed off left, bear right below craggy cliffs towards the relay station. Go left at the far end but just before meeting your outward route, swing left again on another path past radio masts. Approaching a service track, bear left again on to a tarmac path. Continue with it over a stile beside a gate, emerging at the end on to the road opposite the café.

8 Turn left along the road to return to the car park.

Route facts

DISTANCE/TIME 5 miles (8km) 3h

MAP OS Explorer 262 Anglesey West

START RSPB car park near by Ellin's Tower, grid ref: SH 210818

TRACKS Well-maintained paths and tracks

GETTING TO THE START South Stack is found by minor roads to the west of Holyhead and northwest of Trearddur Bay.

THE PUB The Trearddur Bay Hotel. Tel: 01407 860301; www.trearddurbayhotel. co.uk

■ TOURIST INFORMATION CENTRES

For online information, go to
www.visitanglesey.co.uk

Caernarfon
Oriel Pendeitsh,
Castle Street.
Tel: 01286 672232

Holyhead
Stena Line,
Terminal 1, Holyhead,
Isle of Anglesey.
Tel: 01407 762622

Porthmadog
High Street.
Tel: 01766 512981

Pwllheli
Station Square.
Tel: 01758 613000

■ PLACES OF INTEREST

Beaumaris Castle
Castle Street.
Tel: 01248 810361;
www.beaumaris.com

Beaumaris Gaol and Courthouse
Steeple Lane.
Tel: 01248 810361

Caernarfon Airworld Aviation Museum
Caernarfon Airport,
Dinas Dinlle.
Tel: 01286 830800;
www.users.globalnet.co.uk/
~airworld

Caernarfon Castle
Tel: 01286 677617;
www.caernarfon.com

Criccieth Castle
Tel: 01766 522227

Din Llugwy Ancient Village
Nr Moelfre. Free.

Ffestiniog & Welsh Highland Railways
Porthmadog.
Tel: 01766 516000; www.
welshhighlandrailway.net

Lloyd George Museum and Highgate
Llanystumdwy nr Criccieth.
Tel: 01766 522071

Plas Newydd
Llanfairpwll.
Tel: 01248 714795

Portmeirion
Tel: 01766 770000;
www.portmeirion-village.com

Seawatch
Moelfre. Tel: 01248 410277

■ FOR CHILDREN

Anglesey Model Village and Gardens
Newborough,
Isle of Anglesey.
Tel: 01248 440477; www.
angleseymodelvillage.co.uk

Anglesey Sea Zoo
Brynsiencyn, Menai Strait.
Tel: 01248 430411;
www.angleseyseazoo.co.uk

Foel Farm Park
Brynsiencyn, Isle of Anglesey.
Tel: 01248 430646;
www.foelfarm.co.uk

Pili Palas Butterfly and Minibeasts Palace
Menai Bridge,
Isle of Anglesey.
Tel: 01248 712474;
www.pilipalace.co.uk

■ SHOPPING

Market Days
Caernarfon, Sat, also Mon in
summer; Pwllheli, Wed;
Pothmadog, Fri; Holyhead,
Mon; Llangefni, Thu & Sat.

■ PERFORMING ARTS

Galeri
Doc Victoria, Caernarfon.
Tel: 01286 685252;
www.galericaernarfon.com

■ SPORTS & OUTDOOR ACTIVITIES

ANGLING
Sea Fishing
Boat trips for anglers operate
from Amlwch, Beaumaris
Cemaes and Pwllheli.

Freshwater Fishing
Cefni Reservoir, Anglesey, is
good for brown and rainbow
trout. www.llyncefni.co.uk
Llyn Maelog, Rhosneigr,
Anglesey for coarse fishing.
Tel: 01407 810136

BEACHES
Aberdaron
Excellent sand and pebble
beach, popular with both
bathers and surfers.

Abersoch
Sand dunes line a long sandy
beach that is shared with
dinghy sailors. A motor boat
exclusion zone for bathers.
Excellent water quality.

Benllech
A blue flag beach with fine
sands that are ideal for

families. A choice of food and ice cream is available right by the beach.

Black Rock Sands, Morfa Bychan

Long, firm sandy beach that is ideal for bathing, boating, beach-cast fishing and watersports.

Borth y Guest, Porthmadog

Beautiful sandy bay.

Dinas Dinlle, nr Caernarfon

Good sandy beach popular for watersports.

Llanbedrog

National Trust owned. Long sandy beach west of Pwllheli – sheltered and beautiful.

Moelfre/Lligwy

Small beach by the harbour. Coast path leads north to the sands of Traeth Lligwy.

Nefyn

A sweeping bay with 2 miles (3km) of sand. Excellent for watersports and bathing.

Porth Dinllaen

One of the most scenic sandy beaches in Wales with a pub right on the beach.

Porth Iago

Idyllic sunbathing but very small cliff-ringed sandy cove 4 miles (6.4km) north of Aberdaron.

Porth Neigwl (Hell's Mouth)

Wild Atlantic winds and waves make this ideal for surfing. Bathing is dangerous here with strong undertows and cross-currents.

Red Wharf Bay

A sand, mud and cobble beach ideal for walks. Pub and café/restaurant.

Rhosneigr

Exposed beach excellent for watersports like windsurfing.

Trearddur Bay

Big sands and seas ideal for canoeing and surfboarding.

Whistling Sands (Porth Oer)

Splendid, isolated beach. Café in high season. National Trust (pay car park).

BOAT TRIPS

Aberdaron to Bardsey Island.

Enlli Charter.
Tel: 08458 113655;
www.enllicharter.co.uk
Mordaith Llyn.
Tel: 07971 769895;
www.bardseyboattrips.com

Shearwater Coastal Cruises

Pwllheli Marina.
Tel: 01758 740899;
www.shearwatercruises.com

CYCLING

Traffic-free routes include:

Llon Las Cefni – Newborough to Llyn Cefni, Anglesey (12 miles/19km each way). Llon Eifion – Caernarfon to Bryncir old railway (12 miles/19km each way).

HORSE RIDING

Afonwen Riding Centre

Pwllheli.
Tel: 01766 810939;
www.afonfarm.co.uk

Cilan Riding Centre

Abersoch. Tel: 01758 713276;
www.abersochholidays.co.uk

Llanbedrog Riding Centre

Nr. Pwllheli.
Tel: 01758 740267

Tal-y-Foel Riding Centre

Dwyran, Anglesey.
Tel: 01248 430377;
www.tal-y-foel.co.uk

WALKING

Long Distance Routes

Lleyn Coastal Path, Anglesey Coast Path.

WATERSPORTS

Sailing Centres

Abersoch, Pwllheli, Holyhead, Red Wharf Bay, Beaumaris, Trearddur.

■ **EVENTS & CUSTOMS**

Abersoch Jazz Festival

Jazz on the beach every Jun.
www.abersochjazz
festival.com

Amlwch Viking Festival

Re-enacts the Battle of Ynys Mon of 972, Jun (biannual).

Anglesey Walking Festival early Jun.

Tel: 01248 725718; www.
angleseywalkingfestival.com

Criccieth Festival

Music and arts festival, Jun.

Eisteddfod Mon

Music, dance and arts – held in a different Anglesey town each year, May.

Holyhead Maritime Festival

Music and dance on Newry Beach – last weekend, Jul.

Tea Rooms

Ann's Pantry
**The Beach, Moelfre Anglesey
LL72 8HL Tel: 01248 410386;
www.annspantry.co.uk**
Enjoy a proper, hearty Welsh breakfast, jacket potatoes or sandwiches for lunch and an evening meal in this relaxed cottage set back from the harbour. Summer visitors can enjoy dining in the pretty and lawned garden. Sunday lunch is served in winter.

Caffi Cwrt Tearoom
Y Maes, Criccieth LL52 0AG
Tea, sandwiches and home-made cakes in a charming 18th-century cottage that used to be a Court of Petty Sessions. Just off the village green, the charming cottage has beamed ceilings and the tea garden has a view of Criccieth Castle.

Old Boat House
**Red Wharf Bay, Pentraeth,
Gwynedd LL75 8RJ
Tel: 01248 852731**
Set back from the wide sweep of Red Wharf Bay, you couldn't ask for a better view. Sandwiches and snacks are available or more substantial meals, including cannelloni, curries, lasagne and lemon chicken. Sit in the garden on fine summer days or in a cosy bistro-like restaurant.

Sea View Tearooms
**Borth y Gest LL49 9TR
Tel: 012144 51332**
Promenade café serving sandwiches, cakes and simple hot meals, such as liver and bacon. Views from the terrace across the bay to the Snowdonian mountains.

Y Gegin Fawr
**Aberdaron LL53 8BE
Tel: 01758 760359**
This 14th-century building once catered for Bardsey pilgrims. Simply decorated on two floors, specialities include locally caught crab and lobster, home-made cakes and scones.

Pubs

Black Boy
**Northgate St, Caernarfon,
Gwynedd LL55 1RW
Tel: 01286 673604;
www.black-boy-inn.com**
A long-established favourite, built more than 400 years ago using shipwreck timbers. Sip beers from Purple Moose and enjoy the menu of favourites and inventive specials.

The Ship Inn
**Red Wharf Bay, Anglesey
LL75 8RJ Tel: 01248 852568;**
Superbly located on the shore of Red Wharf Bay, this whitewashed inn has dark, oak beams, wooden floors

and cottage-style furniture. From the outside tables you can munch on gourmet sandwiches and baguettes while looking out across the bay. The restaurant and bar menus are renowned for their locally caught fresh fish.

Trearddur Bay Hotel
**Lon Isallt, Anglesey
LL65 2UN
Tel: 01407 860301; www.
trearddurbayhotel.co.uk**
This large hotel dominates the shore of Trearddur Bay. Within the complex, the lively Inn at the Bay offers bar meals in an informal setting, while the Snug is ideal for those wanting a traditional pub atmosphere. The restaurant menu features locally caught seafood and Welsh beef and lamb.

Ty Coch
**Porthdinllaen,
Morfa Nefyn, Pwllheli,
Gwynedd LL53 6DB
Tel: 01758 720498**
One of Wales' famous pubs, with great atmosphere and a truly wonderful beachfront position. Light meals include ploughman's, and mussels in garlic butter served with green salad. Tea and coffee are available. The pub was featured in the Demi Moore film *Half Light*.

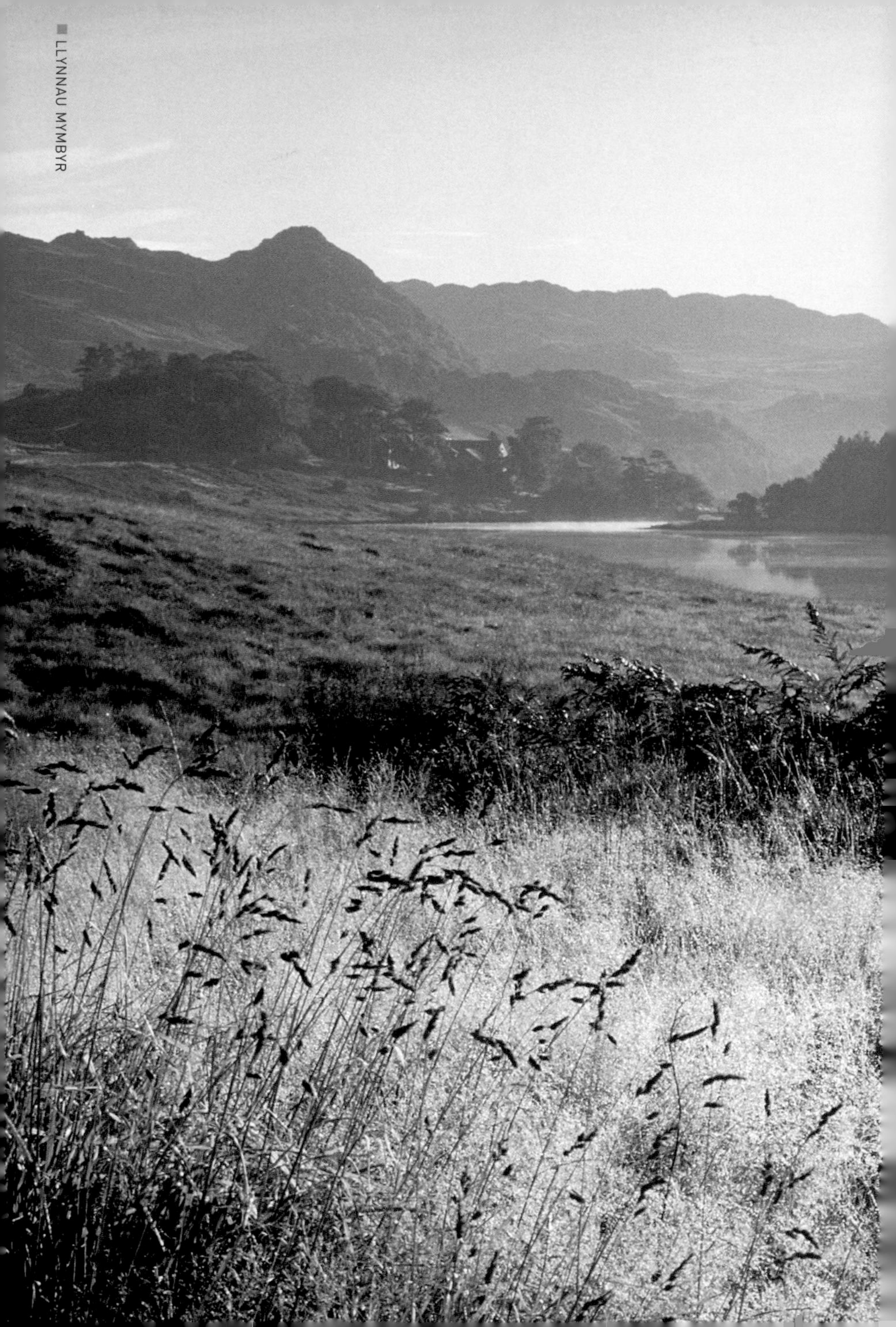

Snowdonia: Mountains & Valleys

Snowdonia has a heart of rock that has enticed generations of walkers and climbers on to its spectacular arêtes and crags, and has provided slate for local building. Here is the land where the warrior princes of Gwynedd scored great victories in battles against the Norman kings, who were forced to build the formidable 'iron ring' of coastal castles from Harlech to Conwy.

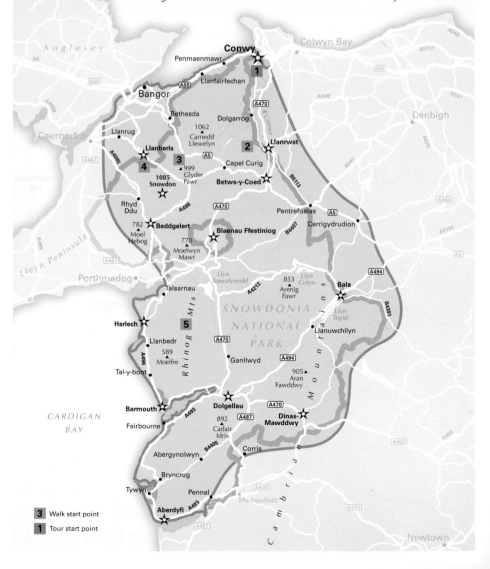

3 Walk start point

1 Tour start point

HARLECH CASTLE

Unmissable attractions

This area has been the inspiration to poets, artists and travellers...visit Conwy and explore its superb castle...marvel at Swallow Falls at Betws-y-Coed...climb Cadair Idris, the most romantic of the Welsh peaks...explore Harlech Castle, which stands overlooking the historic town...travel on the Snowdon Mountain Railway or climb to Snowdon's summit...walk around Bala lake, the largest natural lake in Wales.

1 Llynnau Mymbyr
The twin lakes of Llynnau Mymbyr, near Capel Curig, are only separated in very dry summers. The waters are popular with canoeists from the nearby mountain centre.

2 Conwy
With its two barbicans, eight massive towers and great bow-shaped hall, Conwy Castle is a 'must' for visitors.

3 Beddgelert
The beautiful countryside that lies around Beddgelert in the Snowdonia National Park, offers plenty of great routes for cyclists.

4 Llanberis
The still waters of Llyn Padarn, can be seen from the A4086, but it is best explored on foot on the trail around the lake.

5 Betws-y-Coed
Mingle with walkers and climbers at Betws-y-Coed, the most popular of Snowdonia's resorts, and don't miss the spectacular Swallow Falls.

6 Llanrwst
This attractive arched bridge, built in 1636 probably to a design by Inigo Jones, spans the River Conwy by the busy market town of Llanrwst.

Through the Mountains of Snowdonia

The first part of the route skirts the edge of the Snowdonia National Park, passing through small villages in the fertile Vale of Conwy, before reaching Betws-y-Coed and Capel Curig nestling in the foothills of Moel Siabod. The route climbs to the high Pass of Llanberis and passes a couple of lakes before reaching the coast. There is an opportunity to visit the spectacular Aber Falls, before returning to Conwy.

Route Directions

This tour starts and ends at the historic town of Conwy. The castle here is one of the finest of Edward I's 'iron ring' and walking along the town walls offer splendid views over the rooftops, the pretty Conwy Estuary and Great Orme. The harbour always echoes to the sound of the seagulls that follow the fishermen at work.

1 From Castle Square right in the centre of Conwy, take the B5106 road south through a narrow gate in the town wall, and under the railway. Once through the outskirts of town, the road winds through very pleasant countryside with tidal waters of the Afon Conwy in the wide pastoral valley on your left and the sprawling Carneddau mountains, right. Continue to Trefriw.
Those interested in fabrics might want to visit the Trefriw Woollen Mills, established in 1859 alongside Afon Crafnant.

2 Continue south along the B5106 and turn right a couple of miles south of Trefriw. Pass the manor house Gwydir

Castle, and continue ahead to reach Betws-y-Coed. Turn right along the A5 in Betws, following the signs to Capel Curig. Soon you will reach Swallow Falls.
In Betws there's a picturesque waterfall right in the village centre, and a very good range of shops for tourists. It's worth stopping at the falls, which can be seen from near the roadside, though a walk along the north bank offers a more spectacular view.

3 The next village on the A5, Capel Curig, is the gateway to the mountains of Snowdonia. Take the left fork (A4086) by the Pinnacle Café to pass Llynnau Mymbyr, two lovely windswept lakes set amid wild surroundings beneath the barren slopes of Moel Siabod. The Snowdon massif soon appears ahead.
If you want a huge all-day breakfast or a good mug of tea, you'll find the Pinnacle Café, popular with both walkers and climbers, is a good choice. But if you want a bar meal, then try Cobdens.

4 At a junction take the right fork (A4086) at the Pen-y-Gwryd Hotel and follow the road through the rugged Pass of Llanberis, which squeezes between the highest mountain in Wales, Snowdon, and the rocky Glyderau range. At the bottom of the pass lies Nant Peris, a village shoe-horned into narrow pastures between the mountainsides. At the entrance to the larger village of Llanberis is the massive round tower of 13th-century Dolbadarn Castle, overlooking Llyn Peris.
Llanberis has a wealth of tourist attractions and time demands that you will have to choose. If there's at least 2.5 hours to spare, you could take the scenic Snowdon Mountain Railway to the highest summit in Wales. The fascinating Welsh Slate Museum is situated in Padarn Country Park. Alternatively, you might enjoy a visit to Electric Mountain and take a tour bus to the hydro-electric pump-storage power station built into the heart of the mountain of Elidir Fawr.

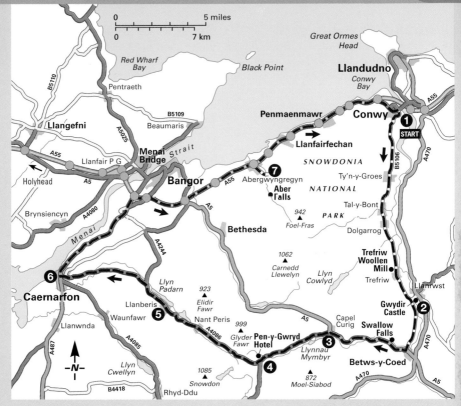

5 Drive through Llanberis, passing the scenic lake of Llyn Padarn on your right, before leaving the mountains for the fantastic coast and castle at Caernarfon.
Here a visit to the royal Caernarfon Castle is a must. Also worth seeing are the ruins of the Roman fort Segontium, which is situated on the outskirts of the town.

6 Follow the coast road (A487) east towards Bangor, just before which you join the A55 dual carriageway signed to Conwy/Betws-y-Coed. If it's fine, and there's a spare hour or so, take the turning signed Abergwyngregyn. Take this minor road south to a forestry car park, which lies just beyond the bridge over the Afon Rhaeadr-fawr. A very easy but superbly scenic there-and-back walk takes you through an upland glen to the Aber Falls.
At the Aber Falls, the fantastic Afon Goch tumbles hundreds of feet down impressive cliffs

of quartz-streaked Cambrian granophyre. The glen is now part of the Coedydd Aber National Nature Reserve, which was set up in 1975 by the Nature Conservancy Council (now English Nature) as an important ecological site and example of a broad-leaved woodland habitat.

7 Return to the A55 and head back to Conwy.

ABERDYFI MAP REF SN6196

In the most southwestern corner of the Snowdonia National Park, Aberdyfi is the finest of Merionydd's coastal resorts. The picturesque, pastel colour-washed cottages, shops and inns, and small harbour are tucked between the steep grassy slopes of the Tarren Hills and the sands of the Dyfi Estuary and Cardigan Bay. Those beaches extend northwards for almost 4 miles (6km) to Tywyn. Besides swimming, sunbathing and sandcastle building, Aberdyfi is popular for most watersports, including sailing, sail-boarding, canoeing and fishing. On most weekends yachts with a multitude of colourful sails can be seen gliding across the waves.

Inland from Aberdyfi, the Happy Valley delves into the Tarren Hills. Its river, the Afon Dyffryn-gwyn, flows from Llyn Barfog, which means the Bearded Lake. Some say that the name Barfog could relate to Barfog, the colleague of King Arthur. Tales abound about Arthur slaying the mythical beast, Afanc, here, and there's even a nearby summit rock named Carn March Arthur, the cairn of Arthur's horse. Could it be more simple, and that the rushes that infest the lake's edge form the beard?

On the other side of the Happy Valley lane the Tarrens proper begin. These superb, grassy whalebacks span some 10 miles (16km) to the Dysynni Valley and offer some of the best wilderness ridge-walking in this part of Wales. Although blighted by conifer forests in places, there are many Neolithic cairns and stunning views of mountain coast and estuary, especially at sunset.

BALA MAP REF SH9235

Bala's jewel is its lake, Llyn Tegid, the largest natural lake in Wales. This beautiful lake, surrounded by the Aran and Arenig Mountains, is popular for watersports, especially when strong southwesterly winds whip up the waves into white horses. The lake is popular with anglers too. Pike, perch, trout, salmon and roach are plentiful, but Llyn Tegid is most famous for the Gwyniad, which resembles a freshwater herring and is believed to have been trapped here since the last Ice Age.

The town is dominated by the wide main street, whose austere architecture is camouflaged by the brightly coloured signs of cafés, gift shops and inns. Bala has religious roots, a fact reinforced by the number of chapels and the statue of Dr Lewis Edwards, founder of the Methodist College, and, opposite the White Lion, a statue of the Reverend Thomas Charles, one the founders of the British and Foreign Bible Society.

The Bala Lake Railway, one of those splendid narrow-gauge steam railways for which the Welsh are famous, has its terminus on the south shore of the lake just over a half mile (800m) from the town. Trains run for 4.5 miles (7km) along the southern shore to Llanuwychllyn on the trackbed of the former Ruabon–Barmouth line. Close to Bala Station, the motte and bailey castle of Tomen y Mur has a long history – some historians believe that the mound dates from Roman times. The castle was one of the several captured from the Normans by Llywelyn ap Iowerth (Llywelyn the Great) in 1202.

BARMOUTH MAP REF SH6115

The Snowdonia National Park borders bypass Barmouth on the side of the Rhinog Mountain. The largely Victorian resort built into the rocks is a bit too much like Blackpool perhaps? When walking the promenade past the funfair and the fish-and-chip cafés visitors could be forgiven for thinking they were on the Fylde Coast, and Barmouth has been blessed with the same wonderful sands. Those who look for more than a beach holiday and who choose to explore a little further, will find true beauty and majesty in the surrounding mountains and the Mawddach Estuary. The Rhinogydd range, which rises from the backyards of the resort, features some of the finest mountains in Wales.

A fascinating web of stairs and alleyways leads from the High Street up to Hen Bermo, the old town, built almost vertically and haphazardly up the cliffs. Eventually you will come to Dinas Oleu (the Fortress of light), donated to the National Trust by the local Talbot family.

As there wasn't enough room to squeeze the main road from Harlech between the foothills and the sea, all roads climbed inland, over the Rhinog mountain passes. Looking down from that perch on Dinas Oleu you'll see their problem. However, in the mid-19th century a coast road was built borrowing ground from the beach area. In 1867 the railways followed, crossing over the Mawddach Estuary on a half-mile (800m) new bridge which had a swing section to allow shipping to pass. The new breed of Victorian tourist flocked here for the sea air, the beaches and the bathing. Hotels

■ Insight

THE ARAN MOUNTAINS

Towering above Bala's lake, Aran Fawddwy at 2,969 feet (905m) is Wales' highest mountain south of Snowdon. The River Dee has its birthplace in a small lake that cowers beneath the summit crags. Once locals mistakenly believed that nearby Cadair Idris was a few feet higher, and, jealous of its popularity, erected a huge cairn to redress the balance. The rocky Aran ridge includes another fine conical-shaped mountain, Aran Benllyn, which is the one that dominates Bala's lake view.

■ Visit

TALYLLYN RAILWAY

The narrow-gauge Talyllyn Railway opened in 1865 to carry slate from the Bryn Eglwys quarries near Abergynolwyn to the sea at Tywyn, a journey of around 7 miles (11km). The railway and the quarries closed in 1946 following a serious rock fall, but a few years later a group of enthusiasts formed the Talyllyn Railway Preservation Society (the first such organisation in the world) and took over the running of the steam railway, which still carries thousands of wide-eyed passengers through the beautiful Fathew Valley, stopping at Dolgoch Falls.

were shoehorned into the narrow strait, built almost into the rock-face. One of those visitors was William Wordsworth, who described the view across the estuary towards Cadair Idris as sublime and equal to any in Scotland.

Artists J M W Turner and Richard Wilson came to capture the changing light and renowned beauty of both estuary and mountainside.

A Circuit of Llyn Crafnant and Llyn Geirionydd

On this walk you can discover two very different lakes. Llyn Crafnant is serenely
beautiful, and it's only 5 minutes from the car to its northern tip. Here, at the head
of the 'valley of garlic', is a lake surrounded by woodland, lush pasture and craggy
hills. The walk is easy, on an undulating forestry track that gives a slightly elevated
view of the lake. After rounding the lake, the route climbs out of the valley, through
the trees and zigzags down into the upland hollow of Llyn Geirionydd. This is a much
wilder place altogether, one with barren hillsides and conifer plantations. Another
lakeside path folows, sometimes almost dipping into the lapping waters. Just around
a corner are the spoil heaps of a huge old lead mine, one of many in the area.

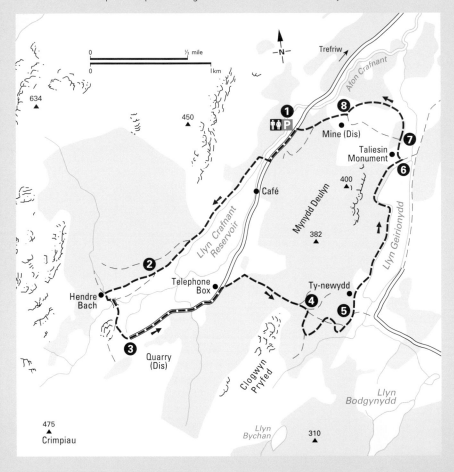

Route Directions

1 Turn right out of the car park and follow the lane to the north end of Llyn Crafnant. Turn right again here, and follow the forestry track along the north-west shores of the lake, before taking the lower left fork.

2 Ignore a stile on the left, and instead climb with the forestry track. Keep watching for a later waymarked footpath on which you should descend left to cross a stream by a cottage, Hendre Bach. Turn left down a track passing a couple of modern chalets.

3 Turn left along the road which heads back towards the lake. Leave this at a telephone box for a path, signposted 'Llyn Geirionydd' and waymarked with blue-capped posts. This climbs through the conifer forests and over the shoulder of Mynydd Deulyn.

4 Descend with the main winding forestry track, still following the obvious blue-capped posts. Ignore the track forking to the right – it leads to Llyn Bychan.

5 On reaching the valley floor, leave the track to go over a step stile on the left. The path crosses a couple of meadows beneath Ty-newydd cottage before tracing Llyn Geirionydd's shoreline. At the northern end of the lake the path keeps to the right of a wall and meets a farm track.

6 Turn left and immediately right to reach the Taliesin Monument on a grassy mound. Descend to a green path heading north towards the Crafnant Valley.

7 Veer left to cross a ladder stile and follow the undulating path ahead over wooded rock and heather knolls.

8 The path eventually swings left to reach an old mine. Here, take the lower track on the right which descends back to the valley road and the forest car park.

Route facts

DISTANCE/TIME 5 miles (8km) 3h

MAP OS Explorer OL17 Snowdon

START Forestry car park north of Llyn Crafnant, grid ref: SH 756618

TRACKS Clear paths and forestry tracks, 5 stiles

GETTING TO THE START
The start point lies 13 miles (20.8km) south of Conwy, off the B5106. Travelling north on B5106 from Llanrwst, turn left along the minor road at the northern end of Trefriw village and reach the car park after approximately 2 miles (3.2km).

THE PUB The Fairy Falls Hotel, Conwy Road, Trefriw LL27 OJH. Tel: 01492 640250

BEDDGELERT MAP REF SH5948

Beddgelert has a location to die for, tucked away near the confluence of the Glaslyn and Colwyn valleys, and beneath the lusciously wooded lower crags and bluffs of Snowdon. The centrepiece of the village is a pretty twin-arched stone bridge over the lively Glaslyn. Huddled around the bridge are the stone-built cottages, inns, craft shops and cafés. Beddgelert and the area around it once made it to Hollywood, for many scenes from Ingrid Bergman's film, *The Inn of the Sixth Happiness*, were shot here.

Beddgelert, which means Gelert's grave, takes its name from the Celtic saint, Kelert. Some tourist literature would have you believe that Gelert was Llywelyn the Great's faithful dog, killed by his master, who mistakenly believed it had butchered his child. The myth and the building of the grave were ploys by David Pritchard, the first landlord of the Royal Goat Hotel, built in 1803, to bring more visitors to his new establishment.

The Sygun Copper Mines, to the north of Beddgelert, are well worth seeing. You'll go on foot on a self-guided audio-visual tour through winding tunnels to see the veins of copper ore in chambers that are coloured by a fascinating array of ferrous oxide stalactites and stalagmites.

Looking downwards onto the copper mine from Snowdon's slopes is Dinas Emrys, a rocky wooded knoll capped with the ruins of an old fort, possibly from the Iron Age and probably used in the time of Llywelyn the Great. Legends tell that it was the refuge of Arthurian magician Merlin, and of Vortigern, a 5th-century British king who was fleeing from the Danes. Access to the area is difficult, sometimes even dangerous, and is not advised.

To the south of the village the A498 Porthmadog road enters the Aberglaslyn Pass, where the flanks of Moel Hebog and the 700-foot (213m) splintered cliffs form a cavernous rocky gorge, through which the waters of the River Glaslyn transform into violent white torrents as they pound the boulders of the riverbed. There's an adventurous riverside path here, close to the Welsh Highland Railway track.

BETWS-Y-COED MAP REF SH7856

Betws-y-Coed, pronounced 'betoose ee koyd', is the most popular of all the Snowdonian resorts and on most days its main street, the A5, will be choc-a-bloc with traffic. Sheltered by enormous hillside forests and sited near to the confluences of the Conwy and two of its tributaries, the Lledr and the Llugwy, Betws-y-Coed is renowned for its waterfalls. One flows beneath the Pont-y-Pair (the bridge of the cauldron), which was built in 1468 at the heart of the village. This is always popular with sunbathers who lounge on the crags that line the banks. The Swallow Falls, best viewed from the north bank of the Llugwy, is a spectacular torrent, lying 2 miles (3km) west up the road, while the Conwy Falls are on the Penmachno end of the village, accessed from the car park of the Otter Restaurant and Café.

Each day walkers and climbers congregate before and after their mountain adventures. There are more

■ Visit

UNDERGROUND TOURS

At the award-winning Llechwedd Slate Caverns at Blaenau Ffestiniog, visitors can take a miners' tramway into the heart of the slate mountain, where a miner guides them around spectacular 19th-century caverns of cathedral-like proportions. There's also a Deep Mine tour starting with Britain's steepest railway (1:1.8), where a 25-minute underground walk reveals the social condition in which the miners lived as told by 'the ghost of a Victorian miner'. Re-created Victorian shops plus a licensed restaurant and a pub complete the experience.

gear shops than food stores. Nightlife tends to centre on the Royal Oak's Stables Bar – those wanting a seat will have to get there early on weekends.

One of the popular visitor attractions is the motor museum. Created from the private collection of the Houghton family, it includes several exotic and rare cars such as Bugatti, Aston Martin, Bentley and the Model T Ford.

Lead played a big part in Betws-y-Coed's early development and if you take one of the forest walks up to Llyn Parc you'll see many of the relics from the old mines. Further east is Llyn Crafnant, a beautiful mountain lake reached by narrow winding lanes from Betws or on foot along a bridleway from the next village west, Capel Curig.

Capel Curig is the true gateway to the big mountains of Snowdonia and as such is considered to be the best-placed resort for weekend mountain walkers and climbers who want an early start.

BLAENAU FFESTINIOG

MAP REF SH7045

Arrive at Blaenau Ffestiniog on a rainy day and you'll see nothing but slate. The houses are built from it, they're roofed with it and their gardens and backyards are piled up with it – great slag heaps that disappear into the low slate-grey clouds. Slate is Blaenau's heritage and they're proud of it. The slate has been mined and quarried from the Moelwyn and Manod mountains that lie either side of the 900 foot-high (275m) valley head where the town stands. When the cloud lifts, the mountains reveal themselves to be finely sculpted with distinctive shapes – suddenly Blaenau's situation looks considerably more appealing to walkers and climbers.

This slate town has its ghostly relics. Take a look at the valley of Cwmorthin, just beyond the suburb of Tanygrisiau. A slatey track climbs beneath the Moelwyn crags past a forlorn-looking lake into a valley devastated by quarries and mines. Beyond the high-chimneyed shell of the old barracks, you can also see the rusting pulley wheels and the bogies of the old slate carts.

Blaenau lies at the end of the narrow-gauge Ffestiniog Railway from Porthmadog, a splendid journey around the Moelwyn and through the beautiful oak woods and pastures of the Ffestiniog Valley. The journey takes you past Tanygrisiau's lake and power station. These form part of a hydroelectric scheme where cheap-rate power is used to pump water up to the higher tarn, Llyn Stwlan, whose head of water is then stored until needed at peak periods.

Blaenau's smaller neighbour, Llan Ffestiniog, is a typical Welsh village with a small square and a large chapel, surrounded by verdant scenery. Roaring deep in the valley, below the village church, are the waterfalls known as Rhaeadr Cynfal, plunging into a 200 foot (60m) craggy ravine. The large rock pillar at the top of the falls, Huw Llwyd's Pulpit, was named after a 17th-century warrior and poet who lived in the village.

CONWY MAP REF SH7877

Few rivers can match the Conwy for true beauty. Its source, Llyn Conwy, lies high in moorland known as the Migneint but soon it is tumbling down the wooded mountainsides to Betws-y-Coed. Here it calms down, passing through lush pastures before lazily meandering across sandbars and mudflats out into the estuary between Conwy and the headland of Llandudno's Great Orme.

Conwy, the town, is one of the great treasures of Wales; a place where history parades itself around every corner. Three fine bridges, including Thomas Telford's magnificent suspension bridge of 1822 and Stephenson's tubular railway bridge, cross the estuary beneath the castle, allowing both road and the railway into this medieval World Heritage Site.

Conwy's castle has the shape we expect in our fairy-tale castles. It dates back to 1287 when powerful English king, Edward I, built it as part of his 'iron ring' to repress the rebellious troops of Llyswelyn the Great, who had given him a great deal of trouble in his conquest of Wales. A statue of the revered Welsh prince dominates Lancaster Square.

Great town walls 6-feet (2m) thick and 35-feet (10.7m) high with three original gates and numerous towers still encircle the old town. The walkway along the top of the walls offers splendid over-the-rooftop views of the castle, the Conwy Estuary and the rocky knolls of Deganwy. At the wall's end, steps descend to the quayside where fishermen sort their nets and squawking seagulls watch out for the scraps. In summer there is a good selection of boat trips, some just around the estuary; others further afield to Anglesey.

Conwy has many fine old buildings. The half-timbered Aberconwy House (National Trust) has origins in the 14th century, although most of its structure belongs to around 1500. The equally impressive Plas Mawr is a large mansion, built for the Wynne family in 1576. Now in the hands of CADW, the building has fine interior plasterwork. St Mary's Church occupies a central but quiet position in the town, on the site of a Cistercian Abbey of which it was once a part; the abbey was moved by Edward I to accommodate his castle.

■ Visit

CAER LLEION FORT
Conwy Mountain forms the backdrop to the town and its castle. High on the hillside are the remains of a much older civilisation, for here lies Caer Lleion fort. Evidence shows that boundary walls surround more than 50 Iron Age hut circles. The walls have almost, but not quite, crumbled to the hillside from which they came. The huts, which would have been wooden, with their roofs thatched with rushes and reeds, have not survived.

A Taming Walk in the Devil's Kitchen

Explore the most perfect hanging valley in Snowdonia, its rock ledges and hanging gardens. If you come on a day when the damp mountain mists swirl in and out of the blackened mossy crags, and when rain-soaked waterfalls drop from those mists like plumes of steam, you will experience an atmospheric menace. However, sunshine can paint a very different picture, with golden rocks that are a busy playground for climbers and small mountain birds, such as the wheatear and ring ouzel. Cwm Idwal is a perfect place to study geology and nature – for here in the inaccessible places, free from animal grazing, rare plants are to be found.

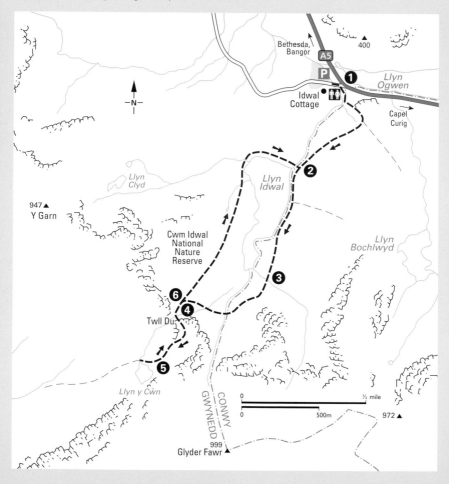

Route Directions

1 The Cwm Idwal nature trail starts to the left of the toilet block at Ogwen and climbs up the hillside to pass some impressive waterfalls before turning right and continuing up the hill.

2 Go through a gate in a fence, that marks the boundary of the National Nature Reserve, and turn left along the side of Llyn Idwal's eastern shores. The clear footpath climbs into the dark shadows of Cwm Idwal.

3 Now you leave the nature trail, which turns right to complete a circuit around the lake. Instead ascend beneath the rock climbing grounds of the Idwal Slabs and across the stream of Nant Ifan, beyond which the footpath zig-zags up rough boulder ground to the foot of Twll Du – the Devil's Kitchen. If the weather, and the forecast too, are fine climb to Llyn y Cwn at the top of this impressive defile, if not, skip this bit and go to Point 6.

4 To ascend Twll Du climb the engineered path as it angles left up the rock face, which will now be on your right-hand side, above an extensive area of scree and boulder. At the top you come to a relatively gentle (by comparison) grassy hollow between the rising summits of Y Garn, to the right, and Glyder Fawr, to the left.

5 Just beyond the first grassy mounds you come across the small tarn of Llyn y Cwn – the dog lake – which makes a great picnic spot. Now retrace your steps carefully to the bottom of Twll Du.

6 Among some huge boulders, the path forks and the left branch heads down to run above the western shore of Llyn Idwal, then rounds its northern end to meet the outward route at Point 2. Now follow the route of your outward journey back to the car park at Ogwen.

Route facts

DISTANCE/TIME 3 miles (4.8km) 2h30

MAP OS Explorer OL17 Snowdon

START Car park at Llyn Ogwen, grid ref: SH 649603

TRACKS High mountain cwm

GETTING TO THE START Turn right off A5 at Llyn Ogwen approx 4.5 miles (7.2km) south of Bethesda, to reach the car park.

THE PUB Cobdens Hotel Capel Curig, Snowdonia LL24 0EE Tel: 01690 720243; www.cobdens.co.uk

DINAS MAWDDWY

MAP REF SH8514

Dinas Mawddwy, a small village just off the main highway (A470) lies sheltered from the westerly winds by the high pass, Bwlch Oerddrws, in a sylvan hollow close to the valleys of the Cerist and the Dyfi rivers. It's a centre for walkers and climbers who flock to Cwm Cywarch where gigantic crags soar to the Aran ridges. The Dyfi valley is simply delectable in these parts. The sleek profiled velvety hills with a patchwork of heather, bracken and moor grass, are mellowed by hedgerow, oak woods and whitewashed farm cottages – this is truly God's country. Indeed it used to be the stamping ground of St Tydecho, cousin of St Cadfan and one of three saints sent from Brittany in the 6th century to introduce Christianity to Wales. The ancient stone church in Llanymawddwy, a few miles upstream, is dedicated to the saint.

DOLGELLAU MAP REF SH7217

Dolgellau sits snugly among pastureland that rises from the banks of the Mawddach and Wnion to the great cliffs of Cadair Idris. An impressive seven-arched bridge, Y Bont Fawr, built in 1638 but heavily modified in subsequent centuries, crosses the Wnion and leads into the market town. Narrow austere streets of stone and slate buildings lead into a large central square.

Dolgellau's origins as a village lie in the 12th century when it was attached to the Cistercian monastery at Cymer Abbey. Very little remains in the town from that period – even the old Parliament building, Cwrt Plas yn Dre, where Owain Glyndwr plotted the downfall of the English in 1398, was pulled down in 1881. The town grew during the 18th and 19th centuries from the proceeds of a large wool industry – celebrated every year in the local 'Wool Race' – and a gold rush of the same era. At its peak more than 500 men were employed in the gold and copper mines in the hills around Dolgellau.

The town had a significant Quaker community at one time. A museum in Eldon Square tells how they were persecuted. Rowland Ellis, one of their number, emigrated to Pennsylvania in 1686, where he founded the famous Bryn Mawr women's college at the University of Pennsylvania.

Come to Dolgellau early on a Sunday morning and you'll see scores of walkers, stocking up with bread, cakes and soft drinks in readiness for a trip up Cadair Idris. Steeped in Celtic legends and myths, Cadair Idris, The Seat of Idris, is the most romantic of Welsh peaks. Though not quite reaching the heights of central Snowdonia, Cadair has all the grandeur of Snowdon and a little bit more – fine crag-bound tarns, sheer rockfaces and wide-sweeping views across what seems like the whole of Wales – it's set in a green, fertile landscape of oak woods, dashing streams and pretty stone cottages dotted across pastoral foothills. The main starting points for Cadair are Minffordd, which lies just north of Tal-y-llyn, and Pont Dyffrydan car park on the Old Cader Road, the start of the route known as the Pony Path.

HARLECH MAP REF SH5831

Harlech Castle stands on a great 200 foot (61m) crag defiantly watching out over Tremadog Bay. It's one of the most dramatic castles in the United Kindgom. Although the outer walls are badly damaged, the majestic inner curtain wall and their great round corner towers are well preserved. Built for Edward I around 1280, the castle would have been protected by what were then sea cliffs (the sea has since receded to reveal coastal plain and sand dunes), while a deep moat protected the rear landward side. The castle kept the Welsh at bay until 1404 when it was taken by the Welsh leader Owain Glyndwr, who then had himself crowned here as Prince of Wales, witnessed by noblemen from Scotland, France and Spain. A long siege here during the Wars of the Roses inspired the famous Welsh marching song 'Men of Harlech'.

The village of Harlech village is quite small. The old quarter lies on the hillside by the castle, while the holiday quarter, including a hotel, campsites, apartments and the railway, spreads across the plains. Visitors come here for the magnificent beaches whose position, with the mountains of Snowdonia spanning the skyline across Tremadog Bay, is quite spectacular.

Behind the village, narrow country lanes wind through the impressive Rhinog Mountains, a range that consists of thick beds of gritstone and shale formed in the Cambrian era – some of the world's oldest surface rocks. The gnarled and faulted crags are riven by deep transverse canyons that create

■ Visit

MORFA HARLECH

This area of sand dunes, salt marshes and mudflats reaches out into Tremadog Bay. The dune system is rich in flora, including the purple-pink flowers of the pyramidal and green-winged orchids. The mudflats in the north are good for wading birds and wildfowl. Polecats have been spotted here, as have many species of butterfly, including the dark-green fritillary. As it's part of a National Nature Reserve, permits are required to stray off the beach and away from the rights of way.

repeated obstacles to those wanting to walk along the 'ridge'. Boulders and scree from the eroded gritstone slabs are frequently covered with knee-deep heather. Early roads, paths and tracks all ran east–west, following the natural lie of the land. The Roman Steps is one such route, climbing out of the valley of Cwm Bychan and crossing the range at the wild pass, Bwlch Tyddiad. This packhorse route (no it's not Roman) was constructed in medieval times and offers a splendid and fairly easy route into these wonderful mountains.

LLANBERIS & SNOWDON
MAP REF SH5760

The successes and failures of Llanberis have always been linked to its mountains. From the moment in the late 18th century that they decided to quarry the slate from Elidir Fawr, Llanberis was transformed from a tiny village to the bustling lakeside town it is today. In its prime the Dinorwig Quarry employed 3,000 men, many of whom travelled from as far afield as Anglesey. When the slate quarry finally closed without warning in August 1969, mountain tourism was ready to take its place.

In Victorian times, popular interest in mountains was in its infancy. Being Wales' highest peak, the tourists' attention was drawn to Snowdon and Llanberis, the village at its foot. When 19th-century traveller, George Borrow, came here he observed that people were going up or descending the mountain as far as the eye could see.

The Snowdon Mountain Railway, Britain's only rack-and-pinion railway, opened in 1896. Unfortunately, the first day proved disastrous, for an out-of-control descending train derailed itself before tumbling down steep slopes. One passenger who had jumped from a falling carriage was killed. Today many thousands of passengers listen to the running commentary as their steam engine travels through woodland and over a viaduct before puffing up the mountain. A sleek new summit station, visitor centre and cafeteria, Hafod Eryri, opened in 2009."

The slate industry lives on through the town's Welsh Slate Museum, which occupies the same Dinorwig site on the northeast shore of Llyn Padarn. Here you can get an insight into the miner's life and his work, watch a craftsman split the rock into fine tiles and see the largest waterwheel on mainland Britain. The museum stands on the edge of the Padarn Country Park, where footpaths climb through woodland to reveal splendid views across Llanberis twin glacial lakes towards Snowdon.

And there's another narrow-gauge steam train to ride – the Llanberis Lake Railway chugs along the shores of Llyn Padarn, from the town centre to Penllyn at the lake's northwestern tip.

LLANRWST MAP REF SH7961

Llanrwst has always flirted with tourism but has never stepped out of the shadow of neighbour Betws-y-Coed. It is claimed that the three-arched bridge over the Conwy was designed by Inigo Jones, and although there's little evidence of this, it certainly is elegant. The 15th-century ivy and Virginia creeper-clad cottage of Ty Hwnt i'r Bont next to the bridge is very pretty and a National Trust tea house.

Set back from the western banks of the Conwy, Gwydir Castle was for centuries the seat of the Wynn family. It dates to Tudor times, but much of the house was rebuilt in the 19th century. The important 1640s panelled dining room has been reinstalled, following its repatriation from the New York Metropolitan Museum.

A few miles north down the Conwy Valley at Caerhun, is the site of a Roman fort, Canovium, established soon after the invasion of Wales under Cnaeus Julius Agricola between AD 75 and 77. The Roman cohorts marched into the hills, tamed the Ordovices tribesmen who farmed the high Carneddau slopes, and built a surfaced road over Bwlch y Ddeufaen, which would link with their fort at Segontium (Caernarfon). Today the platform by the banks of the Conwy is still evident, but obscured in one corner by the building of 11th-century Church of Saint Mary within its confines.

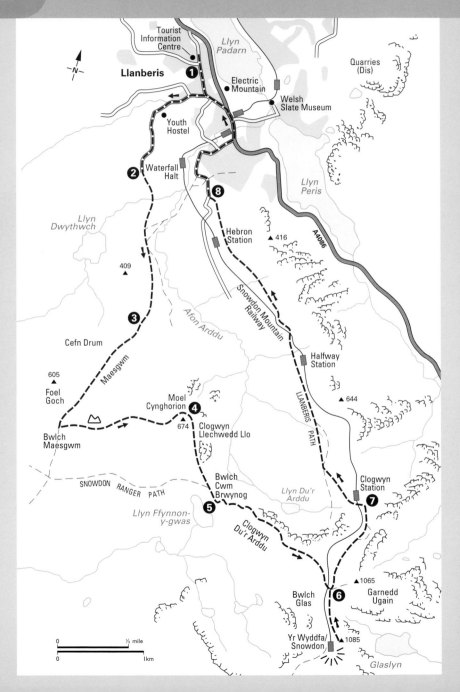

Snowdon the Long Way

A route that takes its time to one of Snowdon's seldom-walked ridges. The route through the Arddu Valley is a pleasing and peaceful way into the high hills. Later on, Snowdon's summit panorama is stunning.

Route Directions

1 From the TIC in the heart of Llanberis, head south along the High Street (Stryd Fawr) before turning right up Capel Coch Road. Go straight ahead at a junction, where the road changes its name to Stryd Ceunant, and follow the road past the youth hostel. The road winds and climbs towards Braich y Foel, the north-east spur of Moel Eilio.

2 Where the tarmac ends at the foot of Moel Eilio, continue along the track, which swings left (south-east) into the wild cwm of the Afon Arddu. On the other side of the cwm are the trains of the Snowdon Mountain Railway.

3 On reaching the base of Foel Goch's northern spur, Cefn Drum, the track swings right into Maesgwm and climbs to a pass, Bwlch Maesgwm, between Foel Goch and Moel Cynghorion. Go through the gate here, then turn left and follow the route for the steep climb by the fence and up the latter-mentioned peak.

4 From Cynghorion's summit the route descends along the top of the cliffs of Clogwyn Llechwedd Llo to another pass, Bwlch Cwm Brwynog, which overlooks the small reservoir of Llyn Ffynnon-y-gwas. Here you join the Snowdon Ranger Path.

5 Follow the zig-zag route up Clogwyn Du'r Arddu, whose cliffs, on the left, plummet to a little tarn, Llyn Du'r Arddu, which sits uneasily in a dark stony cwm. Near the top the wide path veers right, away from the edge, meets the Snowdon Mountain Railway, and follows the line to the monolith at Bwlch Glas. Here you are met by both the Llanberis Path and the Pyg Track and look down on the huge cwms of Glaslyn and Llyn Llydaw.

6 The path now follows the line of the railway to the summit. Retrace your steps to Bwlch Glas, but this time follow the wide Llanberis Path traversing the western slopes of Garnedd Ugain and above the railway. (Don't mistake this for the higher ridge path to Garnedd Ugain's summit.)

7 Near Clogwyn Station you come to Cwm Hetiau, where cliffs fall away into the chasm of the Pass of Llanberis. The path goes under the railway and below Clogwyn Station before recrossing the line near Halfway Station.

8 The path meets a lane beyond Hebron, and this descends back into Llanberis near the Royal Victoria Hotel. Turn left along the main road, then take the left fork, High Street, to get back to the car.

Route facts

DISTANCE/TIME 10 miles (16.1km) 6h30

MAP OS Explorer OL17 Snowdon

START Tourist Information Centre, Llanberis, grid ref: SH 577604

TRACKS Well-defined paths and tracks, 1 stile

GETTING TO THE START Llanberis is on A4086, 8 miles (12.8km) east of Caernarfon. The Tourist Information Centre is on the main street.

THE PUB The Vaynol Arms, Nant Peris. Tel: 01286 870284

❶ Some hard walking to the summit

With the Drovers over the Roman Steps

Cwm Bychan is one of the treasures of Snowdonia National Park and the Roman Steps are one of its oldest highways. As you leave Cwm Bychan the path climbs towards the Rhinog crags, and as it does, its surface becomes one of great rock slabs that form steps. These Roman Steps are in fact part of a medieval packhorse trail, though the Romans might well have used their predecessors. Drovers would have passed this way too, on their way from Harlech to the English markets, picking up local herds of Welsh cattle on the way.

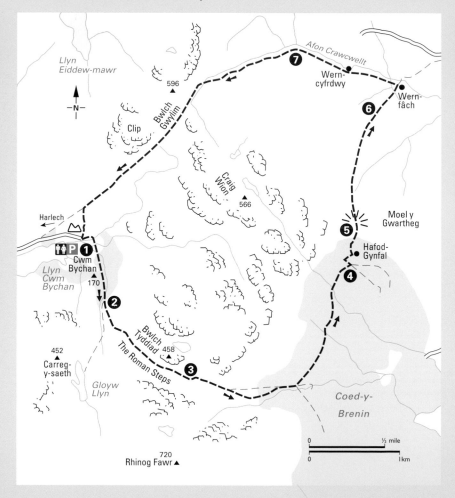

Route Directions

1 Go through the gate at the back of the car park at Llyn Cwm Bychan and over the paved causeway across the stream. Beyond a stile the path climbs up through some squat woodland.

2 Over another stile you leave woodland behind and cross a stream on a small bridge. The path, always clear, climbs steadily to a gate. Now slabbed with 'the steps', it climbs through a heather-clad rocky ravine and on to the cairn marking the highest point along the rocky pass of Bwlch Tyddiad.

3 From the col, the path descends into a grassy moorland basin beneath Rhinog Fawr, then, beyond a stile, enters the conifers of the Coed-y-Brenin plantation. A well-defined footpath tucks away under the trees and eventually comes to a wide flinted forestry road, along which you turn left.

4 After about a mile (1.6 km), the road swings away to head east; watch out for a way-marked path on the left just beyond the turn. Waymarks guide the route left, then right, to pass the ruins of

Hafod-Gynfal. Beyond this you head north to go over a ladder stile and out of the forest.

5 Go straight ahead from the stile, heading north across the grassy moor of Moel y Gwartheg. The ground gets wet as you descend, but it's wetter still further right. You're heading for the isolated cottage of Wern-fach, which stands a little to the left of a small patch of conifers, but for now aim towards the green fields of Cefn Clawdd.

6 You meet a fence, which guides you down to Wern-fâch. Cross a stile, then just above the cottage turn left and go over two ladder stiles. Follow the main stream (Afon Crawcwellt) to Wern-cyfrdwy (house), pass behind it, then join the walls and fences that shadow the stream. These give the least wet line across the sodden moorland.

7 The going firms up as the ground steepens, climbing to the lonely col of Bwlch Gwylim, a narrow pass between Clip and Craig Wion. Descending the far side, Cwm Bychan and the start of the walk come back into view. The footpath now descends

to the southwest, through heather and bracken. After a ladder stile, look for a small waymark where you turn left down steep slopes back to the car park.

Route facts

DISTANCE/TIME 7 miles (11.3km) 5h

MAP OS Explorer OL18 Harlech, Porthmadog & Bala

START Car park, Llyn Cwm Bychan, grid ref: SH 646314

TRACKS Rocky paths, tracks and boggy moorland, 9 stiles

GETTING TO THE START From Llanbedr on the A496, take the minor road east up the valley to Pentre Gwynfryn and then fork left to follow a lane alongside the river to Cwm Bychan at the far end of Lyn Cwm Bychan.

THE PUB The Victoria Inn, Llanbedr. Tel: 01341 241213

■ TOURIST INFORMATION CENTRES

For online information go to www.visitsnowdonia.info

Bala
Pensarn Road.
Tel: 01678 521021

Barmouth
Station Road.
Tel: 01341 280787

Beddgelert (seasonal)
Canolfan Hebog.
Tel: 01766 890615

Betws-y-Coed
Royal Oak Stables.
Tel: 01690 710426

Conwy
Conwy Castle.
Tel: 01492 592248

Dolgellau
Eldon Square,
Tel: 01341 422888

Llanberis (seasonal)
41b High Street.
Tel: 01286 870765

■ PLACES OF INTEREST

Aberconwy House
Castle Street, Conwy.
Tel: 01492 592246
Fourteenth-century merchant's house – one of the finest examples in Wales.

Conwy Castle
Castle Street, Conwy.
Tel: 01492 592358

Conwy Valley Railway Museum
Betws-y-Coed Station Yard.
Tel: 01690 710568; www.conwyrailwaymuseum.co.uk

Electric Mountain
Llanberis. Tel: 01286 870636; www.fhc.co.uk
Guided tours around an underground hydro-electric power station.

Llechwedd Slate Caverns
Blaenau Ffestiniog.
Tel: 01766 830306; www.llechwedd-slate-caverns.co.uk
A tour of the underground world of the slate miner.

Motor Museum
Betws-y-Coed.
Tel: 01690 710760
Exhibits include Bugatti, Aston Martin, Bentley, Bullnose Morris, Ford T and British motorbikes.

National Slate Museum
Dinorwig Quarry, Llanberis.
Tel: 01286 870630; www.museumwales.ac.uk
An extensive live museum of the slate industry. Free.

Plas Mawr
High Street, Conwy.
Tel: 01492 580167; www.conwy.com
This is possibly the best-preserved Elizabethan townhouse in Britain.

Quaker Heritage Centre
Sgwar Elson, Dolgellau.
Tel: 01341 424680
Tells the story of the local Quaker community that lived here, of their persecution and finally, their emigration to Pennsylvannia. Free.

Snowdon Mountain Railway
Llanberis. Tel: 0844 493 8120; www.snowdonrailway.co.uk

Sygun Copper Mine
Beddgelert.
Tel: 01766 890595; www.sygun-coppermine.co.uk
Explore a Victorian mine, complete with stalagmites and stalactites, even gold.

Trefriw Woollen Mills
Trefriw. Tel: 01492 640462; www.t-w-m.co.uk
The mill specialises in the manufacture of Welsh double weave (tapestry) bedspreads (carthenni) and tweeds. Visitors can tour the mill and see goods being made or buy from the shop. Free.

■ SHOPPING

Market Days
Bangor, Sun Farmers' Market; Blaenau Ffestiniog, Tue; Barmouth, Thu and Sun in summer; Conwy, Tue; Llanrwst, Tue.
Trefriw Woollen Mill (see above) and Meirion Mill at Dinas Mawddwy have a tempting array of lovely Welsh fabrics and tapestries.

■ PERFORMING ARTS

The Dragon Theatre
Jubilee Rd, Barmouth.
Tel: 01341 281697

Theatre Harlech
Harlech. Tel: 01766 780667; www.theatrharlech.com

■ SPORTS & OUTDOOR ACTIVITIES

ANGLING

Bala Lake
The lake holds large pike, also perch, eel and trout.

Crafnant Fishery
Llyn Crafnant, above Conwy Valley near Trefriw.
Tel: 01492 640818. Lake with brown and rainbow trout.

DEEP SEA FISHING

Boat trips from Barmouth
Tel: 01341 250341

BEACHES

Aberdyfi
An extensive sandy beach, ideal for families.

Barmouth
Long sandy beach away from the estuary.

Conwy
Good beach with sand dunes 1 mile (1.6km) west of the town, beyond the marina.

Fairbourne
Good sandy beach, ideal for swimming.

Harlech
A straight beach with miles of golden sand, ideal for swimming.

Tywyn
Cobbles with good sand at low tide, popular beach for families.

CYCLING

Coed y Brenin
Huge mountain biking area, with challenging routes and beginners' trails. Cycle hire at Forest Visitor Centre.
Tel: 01341 440728;
www.beicsbrenin.co.uk

Gwydyr Forest
Forestry, miner's tracks and byway routes at Betws y Coed. Cycle hire from Beics Betws. Tel: 01690 710766;
www.bikewales.co.uk

SnowBikers
Guided mountain biking in Merionethshire.
Tel: 01341 430628;
www.snowbikers.com

Mawddach Trail
Multi-user track on old railway between Dolgellau and Morfa Mawddach.
9.5miles (15km).

North Wales Cyclepath
Largely traffic free for its 34 miles (54.7km) between Penmaenmawr and Talacre (nr. Prestatyn).

GOLF

Ffestiniog Golf Club
Y Cefn, Festiniog.
Tel: 01766 762637. 9 holes.

Tyddyn Mawr Golf Club
Crawia Road, Llanrug, Caernarfon.
Tel: 01286 674919. 9 holes.

PONY TREKKING

Bwlchgwyn Farm Pony Trekking Centre
Fairbourne.
Tel: 01341 250107;
wwwbwlchgwynfarm.co.uk

E Prichard Pony Trekking
Felen Rhyd Fach, Maentwrog.
Tel: 01766 590231

The Trekking Centre
Abergwynant Farm,
Penmaenpool,
Dolgellau.
Tel: 01341 422377

Gwydyr Stables
Ty Coch Farm, Penmachno,
Nr Betws-y-Coed.
Tel: 01690 760248

WALKING

The area is the best in Wales for mountain walking. Snowdon, the Glyderau and the Carneddau ranges are the most popular.

WATERSPORTS

Sailing Centres

Aberdyfi
Harbourmaster.
Tel: 01654 767626

Barmouth
Harbourmaster.
Tel: 01341 280671

Conwy
Harbourmaster.
Tel: 01492 596253

White Water Rafting
Canolfan Tryweryn
Frongoch, Bala.
Tel: 01678 521083;
www.ukrafting.co.uk

■ FESTIVALS & EVENTS

Conwy River Festival
Early Aug. Tel: 01492 596253;
www.conwyriverfestival.org

Llanberis Film Festival
Tel: 01286 871534;
www.llamff.co.uk
Early Mar, at various venues – see website.

Tea Rooms

Cemlyn Restaurant and Tea Shop

High Street, Harlech
LL46 2YA Tel: 01766 780425;
www.cemlynrestaurant.co.uk
An award-winning tea shop serving over 20 varieties of teas, along with coffees, delicious home-made cakes and sandwiches. Try local specialities such as bara brith or fruit cake, perhaps on a sun terrace with its spectacular views of Harlech Castle, Cardigan Bay and the Snowdonian mountains.

Lyn's Café and Teagarden

Liverpool House, Church Street, Beddgelert LL55 4YA
Tel: 01766 890374
Sited by the River Colwyn in Beddgelert, the cosy café has a splendid riverside garden where you can relax with a coffee or tea. Alternatively, choose from a menu of breakfast items, snacks, light meals, clotted cream teas and evening meals. The café is licensed in the evening.

Pete's Eats

40 High Street, Llanberis
LL55 4EU Tel: 01286 870117;
www.petes-eats.co.uk
This is one of the best chippys in the world, and, if you're in a mood to be self-indulgent,
look no further. It's lively with good communal spirit among the climbers and hillwalkers who mix with the locals.

Pinnacle Café

Capel Curig LL24 0EN
Tel: 01690 720201;
www.pinnaclepursuits.co.uk
This lively walkers' and climbers' café serves good café grub, including all-day breakfasts, piping-hot mugs of tea and hot chocolate, jacket potatoes and deicious cakes. Ideal for big pre-walk or after-walk appetites.

Pubs

The Castle Hotel

High Street, Conwy
LL32 8DB. Tel: 01492 582800;
www.castlewales.co.uk
A rather grand 16th-century coaching inn adorned with many antiques and some fine paintings by Victorian artist John Dawson-Watson. Dine in Shakespeare's brasserie-type restaurant or there's a popular bar where you can get excellent meals, but be early to grab a table.

The Groes Inn

Tyn y Groes, Conwy
LL32 8TN. Tel: 01492 650545;
www.groesinn.com
Dating back to 1573, the Groes Inn, which overlooks the scenic Conwy Valley,
became the first licensed inn in Wales. A traditional but luxurious inn, garlanded with flowerboxes in summer, it still retains the customary beamed ceilings and log fires. Anything from a light snack to gourmet meals (with many seafood specials) can be enjoyed in the bar or restaurant. Not ideal for kids.

Stables Bar, Royal Oak

Betws-y-Coed, LL24 0AY
Tel: 01690 710219;
www.stables-bistro.co.uk
In an extension to Betws-y-Coed's largest hotel, the Stables Bar efficiently produces tasty bar meals time after time, even though the bar is usually extremely busy. On summer evenings there's a large outside dining area where you can eat under the trees and the stars.

White Horse Inn

Capel Garmon, Betws-y-Coed LL26 0RW
Tel: 01690 710271
A cosy 400-year-old inn with beamed ceilings, log fires and a panoramic view of the Conwy Valley and the mountains of Snowdonia. The inn is well known for its fine food, with emphasis on good local produce. It also serves a wide selection of fine wines and real ales.

LLANGOLLEN

Northeast Wales & Marches

In the fertile landscapes of old Clwyd and the Welsh Marches the sweet shires of England have gently melded into hill country; rolling hills that rise to the high ridges of the Berwyn Mountains and the Clwydians. Hillside fortresses highlight the times of border conflict: visits to the great houses and castles of Powis, Chirk, Denbigh and Ruthin are a must.

6 Walk start point

1 Cycle start point

RHYL

DENBIGH

Unmissable attractions

If it's good old fashioned fun you're after rather than culture, the north coast's golden beaches at Llandudno, Rhyl and Prestatyn await your arrival...visit the great manor houses and castles of Powis, Chirk, Denbigh and Ruthin...cycle along the top of the Dee Valley and enjoy the views of verdant hills...marvel at the waterfall at Pystyll Rhaeadr or the Pontcysyllte Aqueduct, Thomas Telford's feat of engineering over the deep gorge of the River Dee...explore the Montgomeryshire hills on the Welshpool and Llanfair Light Railway...walk part – or all, if you have the time – of Offa's Dyke National Trail...discover Llanarmon Dyffryn Ceiriog, the most beautiful village in the valley...explore the elegant Victorian town of Llandudno.

1 **Welshpool**
The Welshpool and Llanfair Light Railway steams its way through picturesque countryside.

2 **Llangollen**
Thomas Telford built the Pontcysyllte Aqueduct, near Llangollen, in 1795. This inspired construction carries the great Llangollen Canal over the deep gorge of the River Dee.

3 **Offa's Dyke**
The Offa's Dyke National Trail winds its way through some spectacular Welsh landscape.

4 **Llandudno**
The sweeping sands of Llandudno Bay are protected by the headlands of Great Orme and Little Orme.

5 **Pistyll Rhaeadr**
Situated in the lovely Berwyn Mountains, Pistyll Rhaeadr, the highest waterfall in Wales, plunges through a wooded gorge.

Across the Llangollen Skyline

Enjoy Llangollen's beautiful valley on a lofty skyline ride. The Dee Valley is one of Wales' most beautiful places. Verdant hills and a still lively meandering river contrast with the extensive crags and screes of the Trefor Rocks. Although the ride is strenuous on the climbs, the route offers exquisite lofty views of the landscapes.

Route Directions

1 Fed by the waters of the River Dee, diverted at the Horseshoe Falls east of Llangollen, Thomas Telford's 43-mile (69km) narrowboat canal was completed in 1805. For many years barges carried slate and lime from the town and brought in coal from the nearby Ruabon coalfields. Today it is one of the best loved and most scenic of leisure canals. From Llangollen Wharf take the eastbound towpath past the narrowboat moorings. Through the trees there will be lovely views of the Dee Valley on the right and the castle-topped hill of Dinas Bran on the left. The canal passes underneath the Llangollen road.

2 Watch out for the whitewashed Sun Trevor pub on the left. When you see it, follow the exit track just preceding the canal bridge. Through a kissing gate the

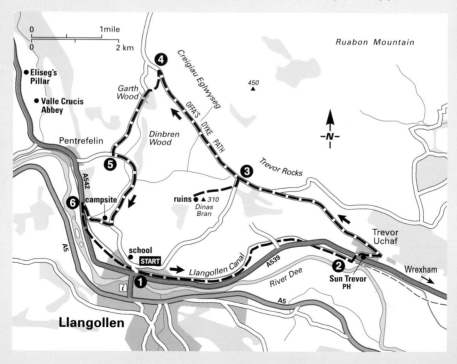

track climbs away from the towpath, before turning left over the bridge to the main road. Cross the road with care before following the lane opposite behind the inn. The climb is steep at first but it steadies as height is gained. Soon the lane is raking over the hillslopes high above the Dee and beneath limestone crags. A lane joins in from the right as you pass beneath Trevor Rocks. You are now following Offa's Dyke. The road descends for a while, with the domed knoll of Dinas Bran, which dominates the view ahead.

3 There's a footpath to the summit of Dinas Bran starting from a narrow lane on the left, and if there's time it would be a good idea to secure the bikes and detour on foot to the extensive castle ruins. When you get to the top, the ruins are large and impressive. The castle was almost certainly built for the Princes of Powys, but you can still see the embankment of a much earlier Iron Age fort. The Welsh castle's demise isn't known for certain, but it was probably laid waste by Edward I. Back on the cycle route, the high lane, which is lined by twisted hawthorn trees, climbs steadily beneath the tiered limestone cliffs

with the rocks of Creigiau Eglwyseg ahead.

4 The views are so wide-sweeping and magnificent that it seems a shame to come down, but to avoid using busy main roads the route turns left on a lane signed to Llangollen. After passing Garth Wood the narrow lane descends steeply (take care).

5 Turn left at the next T-junction, Dinbren Road and then right at a crossroads by Tower Farm Campsite (Tower Road). This brings you down to the A542 after crossing the Llangollen canal.

6 Don't cross the road but turn left along the pavement, then go left through the smaller of two gates on to the canal towpath. This route leads back to Llangollen Wharf, where the café awaits to offer refreshments.

Route facts

DISTANCE/TIME 6 miles (9.7km) 2h30

MAP OS Explorer: either 255 or 256; OS Landranger Sheet 117

START Llangollen Wharf, grid ref: SJ 215423

TRACKS Canal towpath, hilly country lanes

GETTING TO THE START
Llangollen lies 13 miles (20.8km) southwest of Wrexham on the A5 and A539 roads. The main car park, open at all times, is in Market Street, just off Castle Street. To get to Llangollen Wharf at the start of the ride, go to the north side of the Dee bridge, turn left for a short way, cross the road and climb the lane on the left to the Wharf. At weekends there is parking on this lane, in summer holidays there is cheap all-day parking at the school.

CYCLE HIRE Llangollen Bike Hire: Tel: 01978 860605

THE PUB The Sun Trevor Inn, Llangollen.
Tel: 01978 860651

❶ Cyclists are asked to dismount when passing the wharf and moorings area around Llangollen.

CEIRIOG VALLEY MAP REF SJ2037

'A piece of heaven that has fallen to earth' is how the last British Liberal Prime Minister, Lloyd George, described the Ceiriog Valley. The Ceiriog river, which has its birthplace deep in the heart of the Berwyn Mountains, is a tributary of the Dee. Here it flows through a pastoral countryside, dotted with small farms, that wouldn't go amiss in a Constable landscape. It's not surprising that the valley has, over the centuries, inspired three local bards: Huw Morus (1662–1709), the Reverend Robert Ellis (1812–75) and John Ceiriog Hughes (1832–87).

Glyn Ceiriog is the largest village. It expanded in the 19th century with the mining of slate and other minerals in the area. There are still remnants of a tramway that was built to convey the slate to the main line at Chirk.

Llanarmon Dyffryn Ceiriog is the most beautiful village in the valley, with a church, two old-world pubs and several whitewashed cottages clustering around a picture-postcard square. Lying by the confluence of the Ceiriog and a tributary, the Gwrachen, the village takes its name from the 5th-century missionary, St Garmon. A mound in the churchyard, known as Tomen Garmon, is a Bronze Age burial mound which is believed to be the place where the missionary once stood to preach.

CHIRK MAP REF SJ2837

The border town of Chirk perches on a hillside separating the River Dee from the Ceiriog. It is a 'must' for canal enthusiasts who can marvel at Thomas Telford's magnificent ten-arched aqueduct, built in 1801 to convey the canal more than 70 feet (21m) above the valley bottom. Alongside there's an even taller viaduct, built by Henry Robertson in 1840 for the railway. Both were used to carry coal from the once thriving Flintshire coalfields.

Chirk Castle, which overlooks the town and the Ceiriog Valley, was built in 1310 by Edward I's Justice of Wales, Roger Mortimer, to replace an older, 11th-century wooden motte and bailey castle south of the town. The walls have since been decorated by scores of glazed mullioned windows, hiding the stark repressive face those powerful circular towers would have issued. The castle has been continuously inhabited since 1595 by the Myddleton family, whose heraldic icon, 'the bloody red hand' can be seen on the signs of many a local pub.

DENBIGH MAP REF SJ0466

Denbighshire's medieval county town basks in the heart of the Vale of Clwyd, a wide and verdant valley dividing the rolling Clwydian Hills and the foothills of Mynydd Hiraethog's moorland.

◼ Visit

ONE OF THE SEVEN WONDERS

Pistyll Rhaeadr, a remote waterfall 4 miles (6.5km) northwest of Llanrhaeadr-ym-Mochnant, is one of the Seven Wonders of Wales. Here the Afon Disgynfa tumbles 250 feet (76m) from the marshy wilderness of its glacial hanging valley, down tree-clad cliffs into the shadows of Tan y Pistyll, dwarfing the Welsh slate farmhouse at its foot. Most wonderfully, that farmhouse is also a licensed café.

Denbigh means 'little fortress', probably referring to the original hilltop castle belonging to the ancient Welsh princes, rather than the large Norman castle you see today. After defeating the Welsh in 1282, Edward I granted the town to Henry de Lacy, who became the first Lord of Denbigh. The castle and its town walls were completed not long afterwards. The fortress would see much action in the years that followed, culminating in a successful six-month siege of Royalist troops during the Civil War. Though the castle was to fall into decay not long afterwards, there's still much to see, including the gatehouse, fronted by two polygonal towers, and walls that give tremendous views of the town, valley and the Clwydian Hills. In the grounds is the 14th-century tower of the otherwise demolished St Hilary's Church and an old statue believed to be Edward I. It takes very little imagination to conjure up images of how this powerful fortress would have looked.

Beneath the castle, Denbigh has many historical corners and buildings to explore. Narrow ginnels like Back Row thread quietly through the medieval part of the town, revealing buildings from the 15th century. The town also has the remains of a 14th-century Carmelite Friary, and the walls of an unfinished 'cathedral' dreamed up by Dudley, Earl of Leicester, lover of Elizabeth I, but abandoned on his death in 1588.

Denbigh is handily placed for an exploration of the Clwydian Hills, which have long been popular with walkers who delight in the heather ridges. Moel Famau, which means 'mother mountain',

■ Visit

LLYN BRENIG

Llyn Brenig is a 920-acre (368ha) reservoir sited high in the wilderness of the Mynydd Hiraethog. Formed by the flooding of the Afon Fechan and Brenig valleys, the huge reservoir is very popular for fishing, sailing and walking. The Visitor Centre is full of information on the area, including its archaeological heritage. Unfortunately, some of that heritage lies beneath the water, but on the northeast shores you can discover Mesolithic camps with artefacts dating back to 5700 BC.

is at 1,818 feet (554m) the highest of the range. Its summit monument was built in 1810 to celebrate the jubilee of King George III. The square tower and spire were wrecked by a violent gale 50 years later, and the place lay in ruins until 1970 when it was tidied up. To the west, and clearly in view from the ridge, are the concentric earthwork rings of Maes y Gaer, just one of many ancient fortifications on the range.

KNIGHTON & OFFA'S DYKE
MAP REF SO02872

Knighton, a country market town, rather affluent in its appearance, lies on the southern bank of the River Teme, surrounded by lovely, low, rounded hills. The English border, including the town's hill, Panpunton, lies on the other side of the river. Tref y Clawdd, the Welsh name for Knighton means town on the dyke, and a motte and bailey castle in the heart of town stands squarely on Offa's Dyke, an 8th-century earthwork – the only place where this happens.

The main street ascends gently to a fine Victorian clock tower and then on to Market Street, with Georgian houses and businesses with traditional shopfronts, rather than the brightly coloured plastic panels of the usual high street names.

Knighton has the scant remains of two castles, the open motte at Bryn-y-Castell to the east of town, and the remains of a Norman castle, sacked by Owain Glyndwr, which can just be seen at the back of the fire station. Both are now in private ownership. The town is an excellent base for walking, and the Offa's Dyke Centre on West Street can help with information and advice.

For centuries Welsh warlords had attacked their Anglo Saxon enemies in attempts to force them back across the Marches but, in the 8th century Offa, King of Mercia, decided to settle the disputes. He built a massive earthwork dyke running the full length of Wales, from Prestatyn to Chepstow, intended to mark out the political boundary of his kingdom, beyond which the Welsh were permitted only under strict control. The dyke in these parts is at its grandest, with clear earthwork lines straddling the moors. Today there is a well-established national trail along its length. The Glyndwr's Way, another national trail, also starts here.

Knighton is served by the Heart of Wales Railway, running from Swansea to Shrewsbury. This scenic railway weaves its way through the lonely hills and valleys of Mid-Wales and is popular with walkers who want to do a linear route or those wanting to see the Victorian spa towns of Builth and Llandrindod Wells.

LLANDUDNO MAP REF SH7782

Llandudno is by far the most elegant of the North Wales seaside resorts. The Victorian town, whose sweeping sandy northern bay is sheltered by two great limestone promontories, Great Orme and Little Orme, also extends to a west shore looking out on to the Conwy Estuary and the mountains of Snowdonia.

The town's shopping centre is built right up to the crags of Great Orme, as is the 2,295 foot (700m) long Victorian pier, the longest and most attractive pier in Wales. Just beyond the pier visitors can take their cars up the Marine Drive toll road, which takes them on to Great Orme, where there are several well-placed car parks. The more adventurous may chose to walk to the top through a park called Happy Valley and past the ski run. Alternatively, there's a Victorian tram or a cable car. On Great Orme there's history round every corner, with Europe's only Bronze Age copper mines that are open to the public; an Iron Age fort, caves that were inhabited in the upper Palaeolithic period, and a church, St Tudno's, with 6th-century origins.

Colwyn Bay, situated on the other side of Little Orme, was established in the same Victorian era, but hasn't got Llandudno's elegance of architecture. The chief attraction here is the Welsh Mountain Zoo, overlooking Colwyn Bay, a conservation zoo with snow leopards and Sumatran tigers.

Beauty and elegance are diluted the further east you go, but they're replaced by frivolity. Rhyl, which developed into a successful resort in Victorian days, has wall-to-wall caravan parks, a pleasure

■ Visit

RHUDDLAN CASTLE

The 13th-century Norman castle lies just 3 miles (5km) south of the coast at Rhyl. Those who make it on foot from the resort, following the banks of the River Clwyd, will notice that the banks are uniformly straight. The need to gain access to the fortress from the sea was satisfied by canalising the river, a huge project involving 1,800 ditchers. The powerful symmetry of the castle is very impressive, and Gillot's Tower, which provided access to the river below, and the twin-towered gatehouse are the dominant features.

■ Visit

MONTGOMERY

Montgomery ticks over at an altogether more leisurely pace than Welshpool. This fine country town has an elegant red-brick town hall with a clock tower, and a half-timbered 16th-century inn, the Dragon Hotel, is dominated by its medieval castle, established by William I's friend, Roger de Montgomery. The huge earthworks of the Fridd Faldwyn fort were built long before the Roman Conquest. Artefacts, including neolithic tools, are now held in the National Museum in Cardiff.

beach, plenty of kiss-me-quick hats and candy floss – nice if you like that sort of thing: bedlam if you don't. The beaches are excellent and it might just be the place to keep the children happy.

Prestatyn, the last resort before the Point of Ayr and the Dee Estuary, has the hills for back up. Here the Clwydians come down to the sea, as does the Offa's Dyke long-distance path. In times gone by the land around here extended much

further north and there are remnants of a forest, which at low tide has yielded artefacts of neolithic man.

LLANGOLLEN MAP REF SJ2141

This self-proclaimed gateway to Wales sits very prettily in the fertile and verdant Dee Valley, surrounded by the Llantysilio and Berwyn mountains. The river is at the heart of the town and on any fair day you'll see scores of people congregating around the Elizabethan stone bridge, one of the Seven Wonders of Wales, watching the fast waters bursting over the riverbed rocks.

The bridge was extended in 1863 for the railway line, which linked Wrexham with Barmouth. Following the railway's closure in the 1960s, a preservation society was formed and today steam trains operate 7.5 miles (12km) to Carrog. The society expects that it will eventually re-open the line to Corwen. Llangollen station is a reminder of days gone by, with its historic steam engines and rolling stock lined up on platforms that are spanned by the original Great Western Railway footbridge.

The Llangollen canal runs parallel to the railway and road. Pioneered by Thomas Telford, it provides another transport leisure link for horse-drawn narrowboats, which take visitors along the canal and over the Pontcysyllte Aqueduct, where a cast-iron trough carries the canal for 1,007 feet (300m), 120 feet (35m) above the River Dee.

Looking to the skies you can see the ruffled outlines of castle ruins perched on a limestone knoll above the town. Known as Dinas Bran, it was occupied by the Princes of Powys. A walk up the hill reveals that the ruins are quite extensive and the views up the Dee Valley are tremendous – they're far better than the famed Horseshoe Pass, a 4-mile (6km) drive away. Behind Dinas Bran are the long tiered limestone cliffs of Creigiau Eglwyseg. One of the most impressive sights of the region, they stretch to a place called World's End!

Just off the A542 Horseshoe Pass road in the deep, narrow Eglwyseg Valley, lies the ruined abbey of Valle Crucis, a name that means valley of the cross. This was a reference to the cross that used to top the Pillar of Eliseg, a memorial to the 9th-century Prince of Powys. Established in 1201 by Cistercian monks from Strata Marcella near Welshpool, the abbey is sited in fertile pastures beneath a knoll delightfully named the Velvet Hill.

WELSHPOOL MAP REF SJ2207

Set amid Montgomeryshire's rolling verdant hills and wide valley of the River Severn, Welshpool, Y Trallwng to give it its Welsh name, has over the centuries become a prosperous and bustling market town. Until 1835 it was known as Pool; some of the old mileposts still refer to it in that way. The Welsh translation was added to distinguish the place from Poole in Dorset. It was the Severn that brought trade to the town, for it was navigable by boat. The Montgomery Canal came to the town in 1797, part of a 33-mile (53km) system from Welsh Frankton in Shropshire to Newtown in Powys. Today's visitor can find out much more at the Powysland Museum and Montgomery Canal Centre, where there is a V-shaped basin used as a winding point and as a base for the Montgomery Canal Cruises.

The pride of Welshpool's town centre is its High Street, a thoroughfare of fine architecture, much dating from the Georgian era, like the Royal Oak Hotel, but many much older half-timbered buildings, such as the Talbot Hotel and numbers 8–11 belong to the 16th century. A building with a more dubious past is the Cockpit on New Street, which would have been the popular venue for cockfights until the ban of 1849.

Almost every tourist who comes to Welshpool comes to see Powis Castle, which was built for the warring Princes of Powys in around 1200. A long drive from Park Lane off the High Street leads through the fine estate's parklands, past mature oaks and grazing deer to reach the castle. Because of its continuous occupation since 1578, when the ownership passed to the Herbert family, the old fortress has become more of a mansion, with castellated ramparts, tall chimneys, rows of fine leaded windows and fine 17th-century balustraded terraces overlooking manicured lawns and neatly clipped yews. Lead statues of a shepherd and shepherdess survive and keep watch over the many shrubs and perennial borders.

For those wanting to explore the Montgomeryshire hills even further, the Welshpool and Llanfair Light Railway, can take you on an interesting journey through the picturesque and verdant Banwy Valley to Llanfair Caereinion – be sure to take your camera.

Idyllic Valle Crucis and Dinas Bran

From the River Dee to the Eglwyseg, this walk traces a fascinating and rich tapestry of history and landscape. You'll explore the countryside around Llangollen and start by strolling along the canal before entering the verdant Eglwyseg Valley. Later, the route passes the foot of Creigiau Eglwyseg and leads up to Castell Dinas Bran, from where there are fine views, before returning to the canal and Llangollen.

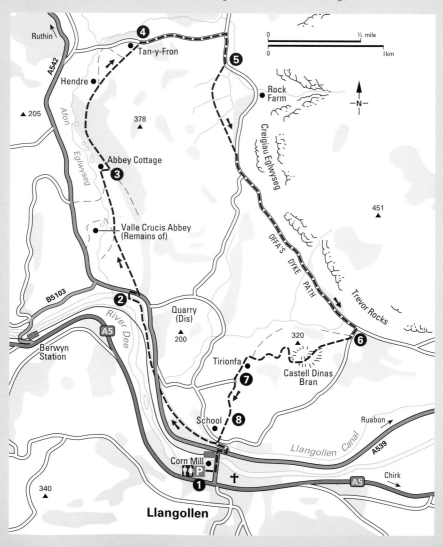

Route Directions

1 Walk from the car park to the main street and go left over Llangollen Bridge. Turn right and then left, climbing to the canal and dropping on to the tow path by the café.

2 After about a mile (1.6km) the canal veers left. Leave the tow path to cross the canal on an ivy-clad bridge. Turn right along the pavement of the main road (A542). Cross the road and take a farm track signed 'FP to Valle Crucis'. The track heads north past the old abbey, where the track ends. A footpath continues, along the left edge of a field.

3 After crossing the stile at Abbey Cottage turn right for a few paces, then left to follow a well-defined track through woodland. When you get to Hendre farm take the right-hand fork leading to a narrow lane at Tan-y-Fron.

4 Turn right along the road, heading towards the prominent cliffs of Eglwyseg, then right again, along the lane that hugs the foot of the cliffs.

5 After 0.25 mile (400m), leave through the second of adjacent gates on the right. Walk away beside successive fields, crossing a stile by farm sheds on to a track back through to the lane. Go right past a junction.

6 When you reach the second junction take the right-hand fork for a few paces, then go through the gate on the right, on to a waymarked footpath leading to Castell Dinas Bran. From the crumbling west walls of the castle descend on a zig-zag path. Go around the right-hand side of a little knoll at the bottom of the hill to join a track near a house called Tirionfa.

7 At a junction, keep ahead to a second cottage, there crossing a stile into a field. Trace the left-hand edge of the field down to a narrow lane.

8 Across this, the route continues along a contained path, passing a school before crossing a road and then the Llangollen Canal close to the start of the walk. Descend the road down to Llangollen Bridge before crossing back into the car park.

Route facts

DISTANCE/TIME 6.75 miles (10.9km) 4h

MAP OS Explorer 255 Llangollen & Berwyn

START Car park Llangollen, grid ref: SJ 214420

TRACKS Tow path, farm tracks and field paths, 5 stiles

GETTING TO THE START
Llangollen is located at the junction of the A542 and A539. It is just within the Welsh border, about 13 miles (20.8km) from Wrexham and Oswestry. The main car park, open at all times, is located in Market Street, just off Castle Street.

THE PUB The Corn Mill, Llangollen. Tel: 01978 869555; www. brunningandprice.co.uk

■ **TOURIST INFORMATION CENTRES**

Knighton
Offa's Dyke Centre.
Tel: 01547 529424

Llandudno
Library.
Tel: 01492 577577

Llangollen
Castle Street.
Tel: 01978 860828

Welshpool
Vicarage Gardens.
Tel: 01938 552043

■ **PLACES OF INTEREST**

Chirk Castle
Chirk, Nr Wrexham.
Tel: 01691 777701

Great Orme Mines
Great Orme, Llandudno.
Tel: 01492 870447;
www.greatormemines.info
Fascinating Bronze Age
copper mines.

Llangollen Steam Railway
Abbey Road,
Llangollen.
Tel: 01978 860951 (timetable);
www.llangollen-railway.co.uk

Llangollen Wharf
Llangollen.
Tel: 01978 860702;
www.horsedrawnboats.co.uk
Narrowboat trips over the
great Telford aqueduct.

Powis Castle
Welshpool.
Tel: 01938 551944
Medieval castle with a fine
collection of paintings.

**Powysland Museum
and Canal Centre**
The museum illustrates the
history of Montgomeryshire,
including its canal.

Rhyl Sky Tower
Rhyl Promenade.
A 240-foot (73m) modern
tower whose observation
car rotates to give birds'
eye views of the North
Wales Coast.

Spaceguard Centre
Knighton.
Tel: 01547 520247;
www.spaceguarduk.com
Join the search for asteroids
and comets.

**Welshpool and
Llanfair Light Railway**
The Station, Llanfair
Caereinion.
Tel: 01938 810441;
www.wllr.org.uk
Narrow-gauge steam railway
between Welshpool and
Llanfair Caereinion.

■ **FOR CHILDREN**

Alice in Wonderland Centre
Llandudno.
Tel: 01492 860082;
www.wonderland.co.uk
Alice in Wonderland and its
connections to Llandudno.

Harlequin Puppet Theatre
Rhos on Sea Promenade,
Colwyn Bay.
Tel: 01492 548166
Britain's only permanent
marionette theatre.

Rhyl Sun Centre
East Parade, Rhyl.
Tel: 01745 344433
An indoor tropical water park.

SeaQuarium
Promenade, Rhyl.
Tel: 01745 344660; www.
seaquarium.co.uk

■ **SHOPPING**

Market Days
Colwyn Bay, Tue and Sat –
farmers' market, Thu;
Denbigh, Wed; Knighton,
Thu; Llangollen, Tue;
Prestatyn, Tue, Fri, Sat;
Ruthin, Thu; Welshpool,
Mon; Wrexham, Mon.

■ **PERFORMING ARTS**

Clwyd Theatre
Mold. Tel: 0845 330 3565

Theatr Colwyn
Abergele Road, Colwyn Bay.
Tel: 01492 532668

Venue Cymru
Promenade, Llandudno.
Tel: 01492 872000;
www.venuecymru.co.uk

■ **SPORTS &
OUTDOOR ACTIVITIES**

ANGLING

Fly Fishing
Llyn Brenig.
Fly fishing for rainbow trout.
Permits from Llyn Brenig
Visitor Centre.
Tel: 01490 420463
Day permits from
machines.

BEACHES

Abergele
A good beach popular with windsurfers and canoeists. Good car parking.

Colwyn Bay
A lively pier and a good arcing sandy beach sheltered by the Little Orme.

Llandudno
Two excellent sandy beaches either side of the Great Orme. The West Beach has a pier and many activities like Punch and Judy shows.

Prestatyn
4 miles (6.5km) of sand, very popular with families.

Rhyl
3 miles (5km) of sand, good for families.

CYCLING

For challenging routes on the Clwydian range of grassy hills www.ridetheclwyds.com

Llandegla Forest & Llyn Brenig
Forest & waterside trails Bike hire:
Tel: 01978 751656; www.oneplanetadventure.com

GOLF

Chirk Golf Club
Chirk, Nr Wrexham.
Tel: 01691 774407. 18 holes.

Knighton Golf Club
Ffrydd Wood, Knighton.
Tel: 01547 528646. 9 holes.

Llanymynech Golf Club
Pant, Nr Oswestry.
Tel: 01691 830983. 18 holes.

Old Colwyn Golf Club
Woodland Avenue, Old Colwyn.
Tel: 01492 515581
9 holes.

Rhos-on-Sea Golf Club
Glan-y-mor Road, Penrhyn Bay, Llandudno.
Tel: 01492 549641.
18 holes.

HORSE RIDING

Bridlewood Riding Centre
Prestatyn.
Tel: 01745 888922;
www.bridlewood.co.uk

Ceiriog Valley
Pont-y-Meibion, Glyn Ceiriog, Llangollen.
Tel: 01691 718686

Mill Pony Trekking
Bwlch Y Ffridd,
Newtown, Powys.
Tel: 01686 688440

Springhill Farm Riding Stables
Selattyn, Oswestry.
Tel: 01691 718406;
www.atspringhill.co.uk

SKIING

Llandudno Ski and Snowboard Centre
Wyddfyd, Great Orme, Llandudno.
Tel: 01492 874707;
www.llandudnoskislope.co.uk

WALKING

Long Distance Routes
Offa's Dyke Path (Chepstow to Prestatyn).
Good walking opportunities on Clwydian Hills, Loggerheads Country Park and the Berwyn Hills.

WATERSPORTS

Canoeing and Rafting
JJ Canoeing and Rafting, Mile End Mill, Berwyn Road, Llangollen.
Tel: 01978 860763;
www.jjraftcanoe.com
Llangollen activity centre.

■ FESTIVALS & EVENTS

Llangollen International Eisteddfod
Tel: 01978 862000
Music dance and culture, early Jul.

North Wales International Music Festival
St Asaph, Sep.
Tel: 01745 584508; www.northwalesmusicfestival.co.uk

Ruthin Festival
Tel: 01824 703832
Music festival, Jun/Jul.

Tea Rooms

Badgers Café and Patisserie

The Victoria Centre, Mostyn Street, Llandudno LL30 2RP Tel: 01492 871649

Here, delicious teas, coffees and cream cakes are served by Victorian-style waitresses known as Badgers' Nippies. Welsh treats such as bara brith and Welsh cakes are on the menu, along with Welsh rarebit, swan meringues and dragon eclairs.

The Buttery

8 High Street, Welshpool SY21 7JP. Tel: 01938 552658

Set in a black-and-white timbered building dating back to the early 16th century, this friendly café is open daily for a wide variety of snacks and meals. Families are welcome with children's menus and smaller portions available. Vegetarians can enjoy dishes, such as Stilton, broccoli and mushroom lasagne.

Honey Pots Ceramic Café

18 Castle Street, Llangollen LL20 8NU. Tel: 01978 869008 www.honey-pots.com

At Honey Pots you can enjoy delicious teas or coffees and tasty cakes and snacks in smart modern surroundings while admiring the views of Dinas Bran's hilltop castle.

When you have had your fill of cakes you can turn your hand to designing your own, unique piece of pottery.

Pubs

Britannia Inn

Horseshoe Pass, Llangollen LL20 8DW. Tel: 01978 860144; www.britinn.com

The popular 14th-century inn built by the monks of nearby Valle Crucis is at the foot of the Horseshoe Pass with fine views down and over the Vale of Llangollen. The cosy inn, which has open fires and beamed ceilings, serves Theakston's ales and a good selection of bar meals, including favourites such as rump steak and chicken Kiev. Children are very welcome, as are well-behaved dogs.

Dragon Hotel

Montgomery SY15 6PA Tel: 01686 668359; www.dragonhotel.com

The impressive black-and-white half-timbered coaching inn in the heart of the town offers an extensive menu with blackboard specials. You'll find good local produce including local Welsh lamb and beef, a wide choice for vegetarians, tasty pasta and game dishes. The beers are from the local Woods and Monty's breweries.

Grouse Inn

Carrog, Corwen, LL21 9AT Tel: 01490 430272

A splendidly sited inn looking across the Dee and the Vale of Llangollen to the Berwyn Mountains. It is just a short walk from Carrog station on the Llangollen Steam Line. Excellent cask ales are served along with a good menu and specials board.

Hawk & Buckle Inn

Llannefydd, Denbigh LL16 5ED. Tel: 01745 540249

The 17th-century coaching inn, situated high up in the hills, is well known for its fine cuisine and welcoming ambience. There is an extensive menu, which uses local lamb, beef and salmon. A creative bar menu includes vegetarian options. Children are welcome.

West Arms

Llanarmon Dyffryn Ceiriog LL20 7LD. Tel: 01691 600665

The West Arms is cosy and welcoming with its beamed ceilings and roaring log fires. Thanks to renowned chef Grant Williams the cuisine is of international standard with dishes such as shoulder of local organic Ceiriog lamb braised in cider with minted crushed potatoes, veg, and a sauce of its own jus.

ELAN VALLEY

Brecon Beacons & Mid Wales

Four great mountain ranges, the Black Mountain in the west, Fforest Fawr, the Brecon Beacons and the Black Mountains of the east, form the spine of the National Park' and many of the sandstone escarpments have finely sculpted northern cliffs and instantly recognisable table-like summits. The Brecon Beacons valleys are fertile, with fields as green and lush as those of Ireland, but to the north the scenery transforms into the wild remote hills and valleys of Mid Wales, a haven for those who are looking for tranquillity.

7 Walk start point

2 Cycle start point

ELAN BRIANNE

Unmissable attractions

Walk, climb or just stand and gaze across the Brecon Beacons' fertile valleys, with fields as green and lush as those of Ireland, or the wild remote hills and valleys of Mid Wales, a haven for those who like tranquillity and a more subtle beauty...explore Hay-on-Wye, a vibrant market town with a rich history, bookshops galore and an annual literary festival...get into the swing at the jazz festival in Brecon...cycle around the Elan Valley, an easy route along an old railway trackbed...visit the fascinating Centre for Alternative Technology in a disued Llwyngwern slate quarry.

4

5

1 **Hay-on-Wye**
The beautiful Wye Valley, including the stretch around Hay-on-Wye, is worthy of exploration.

2 **Llandovery**
A delightfully lush green countryside with rolling hills between Llandovery and the Brecon Beacons.

3 **Brecon Beacons**
Walking is the most popular activity in the Brecon Beacons with over 620 miles (1,000km) of public rights of way.

4 **Aberaeron**
Pretty Aberaeron, south of Aberystwyth, is an ideal resort for coastal walkers to use as a base.

5 **Elan Valley**
The mighty Victorian dam of the Craig Goch reservoir holds back the waters of the Elan Valley.

ABERYSTWYTH & CEREDIGION COAST

MAP REF SN5881

Seen from the pier, Aberystwyth, the largest resort on Cardigan Bay, looks like any other British seaside town, with a pleasant arcing of the dark sand and pebble beach, neat rows of Victorian hotels and B&Bs, and a nice green hill at the far end. But it is a town of great historical importance and with more than a little culture.

In the 6th century, Celtic missionaries set up a small monastery at Llanbadarn, the original name for Aberystwyth, but the concentric rings of an ancient hill fort on the summit of Penparcau, clearly visible from the harbour, date back even further – to 600 BC. Over the centuries the religious settlement would develop into a centre of learning, one that continues today with the university and the Library of Wales. Like most strategic places in Wales the town has its Norman castle, though this one is in ruins after it was blown up in 1649, just six years after it served as a Royal Mint for Charles II.

Many visitors take the short ride on the cliff railway to Constitution Hill, where there is café, a camera obscura, and a superb view of Aberystwyth and the whole of the Cardigan Bay coastline.

The Vale of Rheidol narrow-gauge railway, built in 1902, takes passengers on an hour-long journey to Devil's Bridge, revealing spectacular views of the wooded Rheidol Valley along the way. At Devil's Bridge coin-operated turnstiles either side of the road allow access to paths into a spectacular wooded gorge where you'll see three bridges, one on top of another (legend has it that the lowest one was built with the help of the Devil) and the Mynach Falls, which tumble from a great height past the treetops into the depths of the gorge far beneath your feet.

Further to the south along the coast from Aberystwyth are the pretty resorts of Aberaeron and Newquay. Aberaeron, a more sedate resort ideal for coast-walkers, has stylish colour-washed Georgian terraces overlooking the quay and riverside, while the busy but pretty little seaside town of Newquay is ideal for families with its excellent sandy beach and facilities.

▇ Visit

PLYNLIMON

Plynlimon (Pumlumon in Welsh) at 2468ft/752m is at the heart of the Cambrian Mountains, a swathe of moors, ridges, vales and lakes encompassing mid-Wales. George Borrow, a 19th-century writer, loved the mountain, and sipped the water from the sources of its three great rivers, the Severn, the Wye and the Rheidol. Two corners of this wild mountain that are well worth visiting are the lake filled rocky corrie of Llyn Llygad Rheidol, and Glaslyn, a high windswept lake accessible by car from the Machynlleth–Llanidloes mountain road.

ABERGAVENNY

MAP REF SO2914

Abergavenny, which is by far the largest town in the upper Usk Valley, occupies a large basin surrounded by three very distinctly shaped mountains: the cone-shaped Sugar Loaf Mountain and the craggy Ysgyryd Fawr in the north; Blorenge in the south. It's also well situated as a base to explore the Black Mountains and the Brecon Beacons. Although it took a pounding after the Civil War, Abergavenny's Norman castle is still worth seeing, as is the museum next door.

There's no shortage of castles in the surrounding area too. Raglan lies 10 miles (16km) east along the A40, while the lesser known 'three castles' of Grosmont, Skenfrith and White Castle are hidden away in low, rolling hills a few miles to the east. Along some of the narrowest country lanes imaginable in the beautiful Vale of Ewyas, lie the romantic ruins of Llanthony Priory founded by Augustinian canons early in the 12th century.

For visitors who find Abergavenny a little too busy – they do get traffic jams here – Crickhowell, further west up the Usk Valley, is a picturesque village that is almost as well sited for many of the tourist attractions in the area.

BRECON & PEN Y FAN

MAP REF SO0428

Although the Romans made their home here, Brecon's roots date back to the 5th century when it was governed by the Celtic chieftain, Brychan, who gave his name to the town. Situated at the confluences of the rivers Usk, Honddu and Tarell, the town grew in importance during Norman times when a Benedictine monastery, a castle and formidable town walls were built. In the Act of Union of 1536 Brecon was listed as one of four local capitals and in 1542 Henry VIII set up a chancery here, installing the exchequer in the castle.

Modern Brecon sees the castle as no more than a battlemented wall set in the gardens of the Castle of Brecon Hotel, while only fragments of the town wall still stand near Captains Walk.

St John's Church, part of the monastery, survived the Dissolution and in 1923 was elevated to cathedral status. The impressive old, red sandstone building was extensively refurbished in 1872 by Sir Gilbert Scott, whose finest work is the chancel's vaulted ceiling.

The town centre's buildings are a mixture of Georgian, Jacobean and Tudor, with a network of narrow streets leading off the Bulwark. The 19th-century Shire Hall with its Athenian-style columns, houses the lively and fascinating Brecknock Museum and Art Gallery, while Brecon's military history is well-recorded and celebrated at the Museums of the Royal Regiment of Wales in the Barracks.

Each August, Brecon swings to its own jazz festival, one of Britain's premier jazz events. For those who like old steam railways, the Brecon Mountain Railway puffs 7 miles (11km) from Pant just north of Merthyr Tydfil, into the foothills of the Brecon Beacons.

Seemingly always in view from the town and riverbanks, the Beacons' twin peaks, Pen y Fan (2,907ft/886m) and Corn Du (2,863ft/873m) display their angular outlines, finely sculpted northern cliffs and shadowy cwms to perfection. The proliferation of walking gear shops in the town shows that many visitors come to walk and there's no finer place than Brecon to explore southern Britain's highest mountains.

The Elan Valley Trail

An easy reservoir railway route with a little bit extra added. It's a very pleasant ride on well-surfaced paths and railway tracks through stunning scenery. The superb Victorian dams on the route are an added bonus, especially when the headwaters are thundering down them. Benches near the dams offer a place to rest.

Route Directions

1 The trail starts on the opposite side of the road to the car park, you can't miss the sculptured wooden gate and gateposts by the artist Reece Ingram. Note the carved red kite on the gate. The tarred course of the old railway leads across fields. After about 500yds (450m)

the track bypasses the old railway tunnel, now part of the Radnorshire Wildlife Trust Reserve. The tunnel was modified in 1993 as a habitat for hibernating bats.

2 Beyond the tunnel the route comes to the former junction with the Mid Wales Valley line,

part of the Cambrian Railway (and later the Moat Lane and Brecon section of the GWR). Beyond this the track draws closer to the roadside again.

3 After 2.5 miles (4km) from the start, the trail joins the road for a short distance turning left at a T-junction.

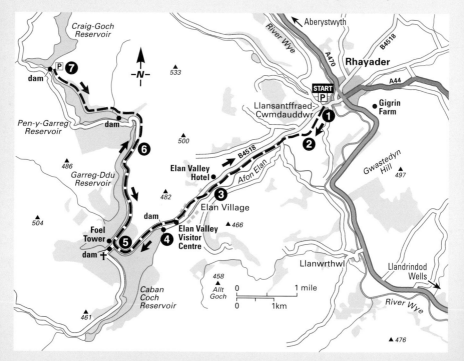

From here you can either follow the road downhill to the visitor centre, which has a café, or cross the road to continue the trail, which soon comes to Caban-y-Coch dam.

4 If you need a rest there's the first of many sculptural benches just beyond the dam – they're at 0.6 miles (1km) intervals and were the work of artist Dominic Clare. The track now runs beside the reservoir with the rock-fringed slopes of Craig y Foel soaring above you on your right-hand side.

5 After curving, the track approaches the viaduct and submerged dam between the reservoirs of Garreg-Ddu and Caban-y-Coch. On the upstream side of the dam is the Foel Tower, where water is drawn and conveyed by tunnel to the filter beds, to eventually reach Birmingham which is 75 miles (120km) away. The submerged dam helps maintain a level sufficient to keep the Foel Tunnel charged with water, whilst the lower Caban-y-Coch lake would be used to discharge into the Afon Elan the mandatory 29,000 gallons (131,837 litres) a day required to keep the ecological status

quo. The track continues past the Foel Tower along one of the most scenic parts of the route – lined by birch trees, and with the cliffs and screes of Craig Dolofau ahead.

6 The trackbed climbs to the road, which should be crossed (with care) before continuing on an incline through trees. It soon swings left to the top of the Pennygarreg dam, one of Elan's most spectacular sights when the foaming overspill waters are tumbling to the river below. You're on the level again now as the track passes beneath woods and through a section exploded through huge crags.

7 The trail ends at the fine 13-arched Craig Goch Reservoir dam where you can stop before retracing your route back the way you came. A better option, however, is to cross to the other side of the dam and then turn left along the road as it winds high above Pen-y-Garreg Reservoir, before descending through the woods beneath its dam. You now join the outward route at the bottom of the incline (point 6) and then follow the track all the way back to Rhayader.

Route facts

DISTANCE/TIME 16 miles (26km) 2/3h

MAP OS Explorer 200; OS Landranger Sheet 147

START Car park at Cwmdauddwr off B4518 west of Rhayader, grid ref: SN 966677

TRACKS Railway track and country lane

GETTING TO THE START Take the B4518 Elan Valley road from Rhayader. The car park is on the right-hand side of the road by the village's last houses.

CYCLE HIRE Clive Powell Mountain Bikes, Cwmdauddwr Arms, West St, Rhayader. Tel: 01597 811343; www.clivepowell-mtb.co.uk

THE PUB The Elan Valley Hotel, Elan Village. Tel: 01597 810448; www.elanvalleyhotel.co.uk

GLYNTAWE & UPPER SWANSEA VALLEY

MAP REF SN8416

The transition from stark industrial landscapes to rural ones happens very suddenly in the Swansea Valley. One minute you're in Ystradgynlais on the edge of the old coalfields, the next you've turned the corner past Abercraf into the magical garden-like landscapes of Glyntawe and you're staring across the River Tawe up to the limestone crags of Cribarth, a southern outlier of the Black Mountain. Glyntawe, a sprawling village, is one of the best starting points for a climb on the Fan Hir escarpment to the highest Black Mountain summit, Fan Brycheiniog.

The limestone geology of the valley has left it with its major attraction, the Dan yr Ogof Caves, discovered in 1912. This is Wales' largest subterranean cavern system, where visitors can enter a weird world of impressive stalactites, stalagmites and underground waterfalls brought to life with lighting and music. The south side of the valley is dominated by Craig y Nos Castle, once home to

world famous Victorian opera singer Adelina Patti. This Gothic mansion, now a grand hotel, is surrounded by superb riverside gardens with mature woodland fringing meres and meadows that now form a valuable part of the Craig y Nos Country Park.

HAY-ON-WYE MAP REF SO2242

Hay-on-Wye lies in the northeast corner of the Brecon Beacons National Park by the sleepy banks of the River Wye, and sheltered by the sweeping slopes of the Black Mountains. With the flower-decked meadows and rolling green hills of Radnorshire in the north, spring and summer in Hay are delightful times.

The name hay comes from the Norman word haie meaning 'enclosed place'. It's known that there was a settlement here when King Offa of Mercia built his dyke here in the 8th century. There are only fragmented remains of the old Norman town walls in the Newport Street area, but this would have been a heavily fortified border town since the 13th century when William de Breos built his castle. The baron soon fell out with King John and was forced to flee to France, where he died in poverty; it's believed that after sacking the castle King John's men starved the baron's wife and child to death. Further attacks and destruction came at the hands of Llewelyn the Great and Owain Glyndwr, and by fire as late as 1977.

Today Hay is a vibrant market town known for its 30-plus secondhand and antiquarian bookshops and tourists come from all over the world to visit the annual literary festival. Among a maze

▮ Visit

WATERFALL COUNTRY

Four streams, the Nedd, Pyrddin, Mellte and Hepste tumble down from the moors of Fforest Fawr to cut deep gorges through the more permeable limestone rocks. They create a series of spectacular waterfalls in the woods north of Pontneddfechan. All are approachable by footpath from car parks just south of the tiny village of Ystradfellte. At the most impressive fall, Sgwd yr Eira, visitors can walk behind the falls and look through the cascading water.

of narrow streets you'll discover many fascinating old buildings, including a colonnaded 19th-century butter market. The town is on Offa's Dyke Path and the Wye Valley Walk.

LLANDOVERY & TYWI VALLEY MAP REF SN7634

Llandovery, known here as Llanymyddfri – 'the church amongst the waters' – was described by the 19th-century writer, George Borrow, as 'the pleasantest little town in which I have halted in the course of my wanderings'. The area was once occupied by the Romans, whose fort, Alabum, was sited near to St Mary's Church by the Afon Bran to the north of the town. The castle, which was built for the Norman baron Richard Fitz Pons in the 12th century, was captured by the Welsh in the Glyndwr Revolts. In 1532 its owner, Rhys-ap-Gruffydd, was executed at the hands of Henry VIII for treason and, in an act of revenge by the Welsh, the castle was destroyed, never to be rebuilt. A recently erected statue of Llywelyn ap Grufydd stands guard on the grassy bank beneath the remains of the castle keep. Across the car park from the statue you'll find the Heritage Centre where you can get information about the many walks in the area, and discover the myths and history of the region.

Llandovery's history is intertwined with the fortunes of the cattle drovers. When thieves made travelling on Wales' rugged roads a hazardous exercise, the local farmers hired the drovers to drive cattle to the more lucrative markets of England and to settle accounts for them with non-local people. This meant that

■ Visit

LLANTHONY PRIORY

A little road climbs south from Hay over the Gospel Pass before descending into the beautiful Vale of Ewyas, where the romantic ruins of Llanthony Priory bask in the beauty of pasture, hedgerow, lovely woodland and the backdrop of the Black Mountains. The Augustinian Priory was established in 1103 by the son of a Marcher lord, William de Lacey. After an attack by Owain Glyndwr the priory was left ruinous, but there are still substantial arches, walls and towers to explore and stir the imagination. Unusually, you can enjoy the view over a pie and a pint, as there's a pub in the grounds.

drovers needed to handle large sums of money and led to the introduction of banking systems some of them even issuing bank notes. One of the most successful of these was David Jones' Black Ox Bank, which was taken over at the turn of the 20th century by Lloyds.

To the south of Llandovery, the Black Mountain (or Mynydd Du as it is known in Wales) lies at the western end of the Brecon Beacon Range, rising in grand escarpments of old red sandstone. Glacial action has formed magnificent cliffs on the northern and eastern faces of the group and also provided two lovely tarns: Llyn y Fan Fawr and Llyn y Fan Fach. Myddfai, which is sheltered in the northern foothills of the Black Mountain, is a particularly picturesque village with a fine 13th-century church.

The nearby Epynt army ranges are encircled by a recreational bridlepath and footpath.

■ Visit

CENTRE FOR ALTERNATIVE TECHNOLOGY

The Centre for Alternative Technology was founded in 1973 and utilised the disused Llwyngwern slate quarry, a couple of miles (3.2km) north of Machynlleth. From very small beginnings, the centre now has a workforce of 90 permanent staff and volunteers on the 7-acre (2.8ha) site. Visitors to the centre can get up the hill on an amazing water-powered cliff railway. They will see exciting interactive displays about global issues such as energy generation and transport, along with some practical ideas for their own homes and lifestyles, including organic gardening.

■ Visit

THE DINAS NATURE RESERVE

This RSPB reserve, which lies 10 miles (16km) north of Llandovery and south of Llyn Brianne, has a footpath over wetlands and through oak woodland to the steep slopes of Dinas. There's a cave in the crags here, where Twm Sion Catti, the Welsh Robin Hood, used to hide from his enemies. Red kites can often be seen soaring above the trees and in summer, you can also see dippers, pied flycatchers, common sandpipers and grey wagtails.

■ Visit

GIGRIN FARM RED KITE FEEDING STATION

Gigrin Farm, an upland sheep farm on the A470, 0.6 mile (1km) south of Rhayader, is an official RSPB feeding station for red kites. It's fascinating to see first the noisy crows arriving on the scene, then the red kites and buzzards swooping down at break-neck speed to foil the smaller birds. The number of kites visiting the feeding station can vary from a dozen to around 400 or so. Feeding the birds takes place every afternoon.

MACHYNLLETH MAP REF SH7400

Machynlleth shelters on high ground to the south of the wide valley of the Dyfi, where the mountains of Snowdonia give way to the rolling foothills of Plynlimon. A fine 17th-century four-arched stone bridge spans the river on the road leading into this small market town. An ornately designed 80-foot (24m) Victorian clock tower forms the hub of this town and looks down on a wide Maengwyn Street, where the weekly Wednesday markets are held. Here you'll also find Parliament House, a medieval town house standing on the site of the building where Owain Glyndwr held the last independent Welsh Parliament in 1404. It now hosts an Owain Glyndwr interpretative centre. The early 14th-century Royal House at the junction of Garsiwn Lane and Penrallt Street is where Charles I stayed in 1644.

Today Machynlleth has an appealing mix of all things Welsh, Celtic mysticism, and green idealism. The unusual shops and the wholefood café are a testament to this, as is the Centre for Alternative Technology. The townsfolk were a bit dubious when the 'hippies' first set up the alternative living centre, but their fortunes are now intertwined.

North of the town, the Dulas valley threads past the Centre for Alternative Technology into a countryside of swift streams, forests and fractured mountains where slate was mined for centuries. At Corris, a narrow gauge railway (closed 1948) is being resurrected; into the hills, hamlets crouch beneath spectacular landscapes, a paradise for the path-finding rambler.

RHANDIRMWYN MAP REF SN7843

Once an important old lead-mining village, Rhandirmwyn lies in the valley of the Upper Tywi, 9 miles (14km) north of Llandovery and the A40. This is a real haven for those who like riverside walks, angling and bird-spotting. Two fine bird reserves are set scenically among the riverside crags, where the boisterous Tywi and Doethie rivers twist and turn between rocky, oak-clad peaks. Beneath the conical hill called Dinas, the rivers converge in a violent cauldron of foam. A short distance upstream, where the Doethie meets the Pysgotwr, is one of the wildest gorges in Mid Wales. Just a few miles north of Rhandirmwyn along winding country lanes, Llyn Brianne Reservoir is surrounded by plantations of spruce and larch in two narrow valleys, those of the Tywi and Camddwr.

RHAYADER MAP REF SN9768

Rhayader's full Welsh name is Rhaeadr Gwy, meaning 'waterfall on the Wye'. The waterfall to which it refers was actually blown up in 1780 to make way for the bridge over the river.

Dominated by its opulent Victorian clock tower, which lies at the crossroads in the centre of the village, Rhayader is a very pleasant town set among some of the finest river scenery in Mid Wales. The poet Percy Shelley was drawn to these parts in 1809. He lived in the cottage of Nantgwyllt in the Elan Valley, then a famed beauty spot. However, the planned flooding of the Elan Valley was to change the nature of the scenery forever. In the first part of the scheme, four reservoirs, the Craig Goch,

■ Insight

THE PHYSICIANS OF MYDDFAI

Llyn y Fan Fach at the northern foot of the Black Mountain is an eerie place to be when the mists swirl around the gullies, and it's not surprising that there's some mystery and legend lurking beneath its waters. From its depths a flaxen-haired fairy appeared and enchanted a local farmer's boy, Rhiwallon. After altercations with her husband the fairy returned to the waters. However, the couple sired three sons, who would learn from their mother about medicine. The boys became the first in a line of Physicians of Myddfai, the last was Dr C Rice Williams of Aberystwyth, who died in 1842.

Penygarreg, Carreg-ddu and Caban-coch were constructed. Nantgwyllt was among the dwellings submerged by the reservoirs. Its garden walls can still be seen when Caban-coch's water levels are low. A church, chapel, school and numerous farms were submerged when the scheme was completed in 1904. A fifth reservoir, the Claerwen, was completed in 1952. One hundred years later the reservoirs have blended almost seamlessly with their surroundings and the power of the dams, and the white waters thundering down them, adds great character to the landscape. The visitor centre gives an intriguing insight into the construction of the dams, the railway built to supply them and the lives of the construction workers involved in the project. The old railway trackbed now forms the Elan Valley Trail, which is a marvellous facility for waterside walking or cycling.

Along the Waterfalls

This is the pocket of dramatic limestone scenery that is often referred to as Waterfall Country. South of the upland plateaux of Fforest Fawr, geological faults and water erosion have produced a series of deep, narrow gorges, sheltered by woodland and broken up by a succession of waterfalls. The highlight of this is Sgwd yr Eira, where it's possible to venture right behind the falls. Walking here is a different experience to that of the escarpments, but the scenery is marvellous and the sheltered nature of the terrain makes it an ideal outing for those days when cloud obscures the peaks.

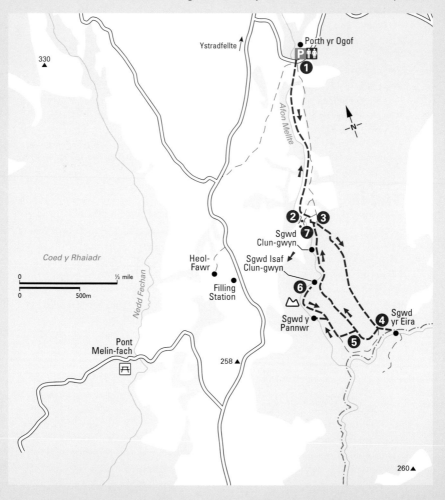

Route Directions

1 Cross the road at the entrance to the car park and head down the left-hand of the two paths, waymarked with a yellow arrow. Ignore a right fork marked 'Cavers Only' and follow the main path through a kissing gate and on to the river bank. Now keep the river to your right to follow a rough footpath through a couple more kissing gates to reach a footbridge.

2 Don't cross but continue ahead, to climb steeply up to a fence. Stay with the path, with a wooden fence now on your right, for a few paces and you'll reach a junction of footpaths marked with a large fingerpost. Bear sharp left on to a well-surfaced track, waymarked to Gwaun Hepste, and follow this for a short distance to another junction, where you should turn right (waymarked 'Sgwd yr Eira').

3 Continue walking along the well waymarked forest trail until another fingerpost directs you right, downhill. Follow this track to the edge of the forest and then bear around to the right. This track leads to the top of a set of wooden steps, on the left.

4 Go down the steps to Sgwd yr Eira (Waterfall of the Snow) and then, having edged along the bank and walked behind the falls (waterproofs recommended), retrace your steps back up to the edge of the wood. Turn left and continue, still following the red-banded posts, to a fork marked with another fingerpost.

5 Turn left here (waymarked to Sgwd Isaf Clun-gwyn) and descend to the riverside. Turn left again to Sgwd y Pannwr (Fullers Falls), then turn around to walk upstream to Sgwd Clun-gwyn Isaf (Lower Waterfall of the White Meadow). Take care, the ground is very steep and rough around the best viewpoint.

6 Retrace your steps downstream to your original descent path and turn left to climb back up to the fork at the top. Turn left and follow the red-banded waymarkers along to Sgwd Clun-gwyn Isaf, where there's a fenced viewing area. From here, continue along the main trail to the place where you split off earlier.

7 Drop back down to the footbridge and continue along the river bank to Porth yr Ogof. Adjacent to here is a spectacular cavern entrance where the river Mellte disappears underground.

Route facts

DISTANCE/TIME 4 miles (6.4km) 2h

MAP OS Explorer OL12 Brecon Beacons National Park, Western & Central areas

START Car park at Porth yr Ogof, near Ystradfellte, grid ref: SN 928124

TRACKS Riverside paths, some rough sections and steps, no stiles

GETTING TO THE START From Glynneath, 10 miles (16km) northeast of Neath on the A465, take the B4242 and then a minor road through Pontnêddféchan to Ystradfellte. Just south of the hamlet, a minor road to the right leads to the car park.

THE PUB The Old White Horse Inn, Pontnêdd Féchan. Tel: 01639 721219

❶ Some steep, uneven sections. Waterproofs recommended if walking behind the falls.

■ TOURIST INFORMATION CENTRES

Abergavenny
Swan Meadow.
Tel: 01873 853254

Aberystwyth
Terrace Road.
Tel: 01970 612125

Brecon
Cattle Market Car Park.
Tel: 01874 622485

Hay-on-Wye
Oxford Road.
Tel: 01497 820144

Llandovery
Heritage Centre, Kings Road.
Tel: 01550 720693

Llandrindod Wells
Old Town Hall, Memorial
Gardens. Tel: 01597 822600

Machynlleth
Canolfan Owain Glyndwr.
Tel: 01654 702401

Rhayader
The Leisure Centre, North
Street. Tel: 01597 810591

■ PLACES OF INTEREST

Brecon Cathedral
Cathedral Close, Brecon,
Powys. Tel: 01874 623857;
www.breconcathedral.org.uk

Carreg Cennen Castle
Trapp, Nr Llandeilo.
Tel: 01558 822291. Perhaps
Wales' most spectacularly
sited castle.

Centre for Alternative Technology
Machynlleth. Tel: 01654
705950; www.cat.org.uk

See some of the solutions to
the challenges facing Earth.

Ceredigion Museum and Coliseum Gallery
Coliseum,Terrace Road,
Aberystwyth, Dyfed.
Tel: 01970 633088
Historic objects including the
furniture, archaeology,
agriculture, seafaring and
lead mining industries of the
people of Ceredigion.

Dan-yr-Ogof Showcaves
Brecon Rd, Penycae.
Tel: 01639 730284;
www.showcaves.co.uk
Visit the underground world
of stalagmites, stalactites,
waterfalls, a museum and the
dinosaur park.

Dinas Nature Reserve
Rhandirmwyn.
RSPB reserve with beautiful
walk and shop/information
centre. Charge for car park.

Dolaucothi Gold Mines
Pumpsaint, Llanwrda
Carmarthenshire. (Site off
A482 between Lampeter and
Llanwrda.) Tel: 01558 650177
Free for NT members only
(excludes underground tour).
The only known Roman gold
mine in the UK.

Gigrin Farm Kite Feeding Station
South St, Rhayader.
Tel: 01597 810243;
www.gigrin.co.uk
See the rare bird of prey, the
red kite.

National Cycle Collection
The Automobile Palace,
Temple Street, Llandrindod
Wells. Tel: 01597 825531;
www.cyclemuseum.org.uk
Boneshakers, penny farthings
and modern bikes.

National Library of Wales
Penglais, Aberystwyth.
Tel: 01970 623816. Includes
exhibitions (some free),
cinema and a restaurant.

■ FOR CHILDREN

Borth Animalarium
North of Aberystwyth.
Tel: 01970 871224;
www.animalarium.co.uk
A rescue zoo for unwanted
exotic animals.

Brecon Mountain Railway
Pant Station, Merthyr Tydfil.
Tel: 01685 722988; www.
breconmountainrailway.co.uk
A narrow-gauge steam line.

Vale of Rheidol Railway
Park Avenue, Aberystwyth.
Tel: 01970 625819;
www.rheidolrailway.co.uk
One of the Great Little Trains
of Wales.

■ SHOPPING

Market Days
Abergavenny, Tue; Farmers
market, 2nd and 4th Thu of
month; Aberystwyth, 1st and
3rd Sat of the month; Brecon,
Tue and Fri; Hay-on-Wye,
Thu; Lampeter, alternate Fri;
Llandovery, Farmers market

last Sat; Llandrindod Wells, Fri. Farmers market last Thu am of the month); Llanidloes, Sat; Machynlleth, Wed.

■ PERFORMING ARTS
Aberystwyth Arts Centre
The University of Wales, Aberystwyth, Penglais Campus, Aberystwyth. Tel: 01970 623232; www. aberystwythartscentre.co.uk
The Tabernacle
Penrallt St, Machynlleth, Powys. Tel: 01654 703355; www.momawales.co.uk
Theatr Brycheiniog
Canal Wharf, Brecon. Tel: 01874 611622
Theatr Hafren
Llanidloes Rd, Newtown, SY16 4HX. Tel: 01686 625007; www.theatrhafren.com

■ SPORTS & OUTDOOR ACTIVITIES
ANGLING
Freshwater
Opportunities for fishing on farms, lakes and rivers, including the Clwydog Reservoir near Llanidloes, the Beacons Reservoir and the River Tawe in. Permits and licences are available from tackle shops and TICs.
BOAT TRIPS
Brecon Park Day Boats
Brecon. Tel: 0800 612 2890; www.beaconparkdayboats. co.uk

Self-drive on Monmouthshire & Brecon Canal
New Quay Boat Trips
New Quay. Tel: 01545 560800; www.newquayboattrips.co.uk
Watch dolphins, seals and other sealife in Cardigan Bay
CANOEING
Glasbury-on-Wye. Tel: 01497 847213; www.wyevalleycanoes.co.uk
CYCLING
Cycle Routes
Taff Trail (Cardiff to Brecon Beacons).
Elan Valley Trail (Rhayader to Elan Reservoirs).
Ystwyth Trail (Aberystwyth to Tregaron, 21 miles)
Nant yr Arian Forest (Aberystwyth)
Cycle Hire
Three Cocks. Tel: 01497 847897; www.blackmountain.co.uk
Brecon. Tel: 01874 610071; www.bikesandhikes.co.uk
GOLF
Borth & Ynyslas Golf Club
Aer y Mor, Borth. Tel: 01970 871202. 18 holes.
Cradoc Golf Club
Penoyre Park, Cradoc, Brecon. Tel: 01874 623658 18 holes.
Machynlleth Golf Club
Newtown Rd, Machynlleth. Tel: 01654 702000. 9 holes.
Rhosgoch Golf Club
Rhosgoch, Builth Wells. Tel: 01497 851251. 18 holes.

St Idloes Golf Club
Trefeglwys Rd, Llanidloes. Tel: 01686 412559. 9 holes.
HORSE RIDING
Cantref Riding Centre
Cantref, Brecon. Tel: 01874 665223; www.cantref.com
Mills Bros
New Court, Felindre, Three Cocks, Brecon. Tel: 01497 847285
Underhill Riding Stables
Underhill Farm, Dolau, Llandrindod Wells. Tel: 01597 851890
WALKING
Long Distance Routes
The Beacons Way.
Glyndwr's Way.
Offa's Dyke Path.
Wye Valley Walk.

■ FESTIVALS & EVENTS
Brecon Jazz festival
Tel: 0870 990 1299; www.breconjazz.org mid-Aug.
Hay Festival
Tel: 01497 822629; www.hayfestival.co.uk
Literary festival, end May to early Jun.
Musicfest Aberystwyth
Displays, music and dancing www.aberfest.org, end Jul.
Royal Welsh Show
Builth Wells. Tel: 01982 553683; www.rwas.co.uk
Agricultural show, mid to end Jul.

Tea Rooms

Giglios Coffee Shop
10 Bethel Square, Brecon
LD3 7JP. Tel: 01874 625062
A modern licensed coffee
shop and restaurant in the
heart of Brecon. Excellent
cream teas, gateaux and
sandwiches, such as smoked
salmon and cream cheese,
Thai green chicken, or
salmon with dill mayonnaise.

The Granary
20, Broad Street,
Hay-on-Wye HR3 5DB
Tel: 01497 820790
The splendid licensed café
has a cosy bistro-style
interior with outside tables
looking across to the town's
Victorian clocktower. Food
includes sandwiches, jacket
potatoes and warming soups
as well as full main meals.

Hive on the Quay
Aberaeron, Ceredigion
SA46 0BT
Tel: 01545 570445;
www.hiveonthequay.co.uk
On the picturesque harbour
and close to the Ceredigion
Coastal Footpath; a chance to
work up an appetite for a
ploughman's with local
cheeses, a savoury stuffed
pancake, home-made honey
ice cream or a local fish
chowder. Boats based at the
port land Cardigan Bay crab

and lobster for the renowned
sourdough sandwiches, while
in the summer, mackerel is
fresh-grilled.

The Quarry Shop and Café
Maengwyn St Machynlleth
SY20 8EB. Tel: 01654 702624
A very popular wholefood
vegetarian café set up by the
Centre for Alternative
Technology. They only use
seasonal, organic and
Fairtrade produce. Their date
slices are absolutely delicious
and the soups will warm you.

Pubs

Harbourmaster Hotel
Aberaeron SA46 0BA
Tel: 01545 570755;
www.harbour-master.com
The hotel restaurant prides
itself on its use of local
produce, including Aberaeron
prawns and mackerel,
Cardigan Bay crab and
lobster, Welsh Black beef and
venison. All this plus Welsh
microbrewery beers and a
good bin of wines.

Kilvert's Hotel
The Bull Ring, Hay-on-Wye
HR3 5AG. Tel: 01497 821042;
www.kilverts.co.uk
The ivy-clad Georgian free
house is popular with locals
and tourists alike, with a
small flagged outdoor terrace

area in the front, a rustic
oak-beamed bar serving real
ales such as Breconshire
Brewery's Kilvert's Gold,
along with bar meals like
slow-roasted Welsh lamb,
pizzas and pastas. The
elegant restaurant
specialises in lamb and fish.

Harp Inn
Old Radnor LD8 2RH
Tel: 01544 350655;
www.harpinnradnor.co.uk
In beautiful countryside close
to Hergest Ridge, this
renovated 15th-century Welsh
longhouse is a classic village
inn, all flagstones, fires,
beams and settles. Popular
with pony-trekkers for beers
from Bishop's Castle or
Ludlow breweries; a great
menu of classics and modern
dishes seals the deal here.

Royal Oak
Rhandirmwyn, Llandovery
SA20 0NY. Tel: 01550 760201
A proper old-fashioned
country pub overlooking the
Tywi Valley and mountains.
Stone and tile floors and an
open fire give the bar a rustic
atmosphere, while the
restaurant is decorated in
cottage style. In summer
there's a pleasant garden.
Meals include venison
casserole, Welsh black beef
and chicken curry.

Pembrokeshire

In Welsh Pen-Fro means land's end and, fittingly, Pembrokeshire's sinuous coastline reaches out into the waves of the Atlantic Ocean like a gnarled fist. Volcanic eruptions and earth movements have left a tortured rocky coastline of some 160 miles (260km), whose beauty and drama have been recognised by National Park status. In Pembrokeshire you can take it easy on the sandy beaches, make sport out of those Atlantic waves, or discover the mysteries of St David's or the ancient Preseli Hills.

8 Walk start point

2 Tour start point

WHITESANDS BAY

SOLVA

Unmissable attractions

Explore Milford Haven, described by Admiral Lord Nelson as one of the world's finest harbours...walk across the Preseli Hills and look out for the famous blue dolomite stones that were transported from here to Wiltshire to build Stonehenge or seek out Pentre Ifan, Britain's largest and best preserved burial chamber...explore St David's, Britain's smallest city...enjoy fantastic walking and birdwatching around the Marloes Peninsula...or take a ferry trip to Skomer's Island from Martin's Haven and relish the views of puffins, dolphins and, possibly, basking sharks...experience Fishguard's Music Fesival in June or Tenby's Arts Festival in September...discover Solva, one of Pembrokeshire's most picturesque and popular resorts.

4

1 **Pembroke**
Magnificent Pembroke Castle occupies a commanding position between two tidal inlets.

2 **Tenby**
Boats trips from Tenby harbour offer the chance to see grey seals.

3 **Marloes Sands**
This spectacular beach, in sight of Skomer and Skokholm Islands, is cared for by the National Trust.

4 **Pentre Ifan**
The precarious-looking capstone of Pentre Ifan balances on three uprights forming the neolithic burial chamber.

5 **Milford Haven**
The Milford Haven estuary proves a safe anchorage for all types of leisure craft.

5

HAVERFORDWEST & ST BRIDES BAY MAP REF SM9515

Sited on the Western Cleddau, one of the two wide rivers that flow into the Milford Haven, Haverfordwest was, before the arrival of the railways, a thriving port with barges, small steamships and coasting vessels regularly docking on the quayside. The castle, built by the first Earl of Pembroke, Gilbert de Clare in the 12th century, dominates the town from a lofty crag above the river. As a Norman stronghold, Haverfordwest was attacked and burned to the ground by Llywelyn the Great, but the castle survived, as it did when besieged in 1405 by another Prince of Wales, Owain Glyndwr. However, Oliver Cromwell ordered its destruction following the Civil War. The substantial walls and keep are still an impressive sight though – second only to Pembroke in this region.

■ Visit

SKOMER

There's also a summer ferry (not Mondays) to Skomer Island from Martin's Haven on the headland west of Marloes. On the short voyage you may be lucky enough to see porpoises and dolphins, or even a basking shark. You'll almost certainly see some of the 6,000 breeding pairs of puffins peeping from their burrows. Like much of the mainland Skomer Island is girt with dark volcanic cliffs, which accommodate southern Britain's largest colony of nesting seabirds. On the pink thrift and sea campion-decked clifftops are the remnants of an Iron Age civilisation – a standing stone, burial cairns, ancient field boundaries and the earthworks of hut circles. A number of footpaths criss-cross the island. Do not stray off the paths.

Today Haverfordwest is a thriving market town, the principal shopping centre for the area. Many shops and a café line the quayside. It's worth a visit to the town museum, which is housed in the castle off Church Street. Also worth seeing are the recently excavated ruins of the Augustinian Priory of St Mary and St Thomas the Martyr, a short walk from the town centre.

Haverfordwest is an excellent base from which to explore Pembrokeshire's West Coast and St Brides Bay. Facing west to the Atlantic, most of the St Brides beaches are exposed to the prevailing winds. This whips up the surf and makes them extremely popular for sports such as surfing, windsurfing and kite-surfing. The most northerly of these is Newgale Sands, where a splendid golden beach stretches 2 miles (3km) from Newgale village in the north to the rocks of Rickets Head. A tall shingle bank separates the beach from the village. Patrolling lifeguards designate the safe swimming areas.

There's another long sandy beach at Broadhaven, a lively resort with a good range of facilities. It's worth exploring the northern end to see natural rock arches and stacks. To the south lies Little Haven. This pretty village with a slipway, used by the lifeboat, and beach, is a popular place with sea anglers.

Most spectacular is Marloes Sands where violent earth movements thrust up the rock strata to form steeply angled rocky cliffs that resemble the yacht sails caught in a great gust of wind. Marloes village is a 0.6-mile (1km) walk from the isolated sandy beach.

MILFORD HAVEN

MAP REF SM9005

'It's one of the world's finest harbours,' Admiral Lord Nelson claimed as he gazed admiringly across the vast blue waters of Milford Haven. And this lovely sheltered estuary has provided one of Britain's most important maritime strongholds since the days of the Tudor kings. And yet Milford Haven the town is a more recent affair, built and planned in the late 18th century by Sir William Hamilton, the husband of Nelson's mistress, Emma. In the 1960s the big ships arrived – carrying crude oil for processing in new refineries. Of these, only the Texaco plant now survives. Today Milford boasts a pleasant harbour front and marina, overlooked by the Georgian buildings of Hamilton Terrace. In 1991 memories were rekindled when the Tall Ships Race came to town.

NEWPORT MAP REF SN0539

While its next-door neighbour Fishguard is bustling with cars and lorries rushing to make the ferry to Ireland on time, life in little Newport, tucked away in the far northwest corner of Pembrokeshire, chugs along at a more relaxed pace. Here the distinctive crag-topped Carn Ingli ('Angel Mountain') rises from the back gardens of the villagers' cottages, while small boats bobble from their moorings or lean against the sandbars of the Nevern Estuary. Although only 1,138-feet (347m) high Carn Ingli is distinctively rugged and its cloak of heather and gorse is capped by jagged outcrops of dolerite. The ramparts that remain from an Iron Age fort ring the

■ Visit

BURIAL CROMLECH

Pentre Ifan is probably the finest example of a neolithic burial cromlech in Wales. It dates back to around 3500 BC and its huge capstone measures more than 16 feet (5m) long poised on three 8-foot (2.5m) uprights, which seem to frame and capture Carn Ingli's mystical outlines to perfection. The cromlech can be accessed free of charge and is well signposted from the A487 east of Newport and the B4329 Preseli road at Brynberian. Near by is Castell Henllys Iron Age Fort.

summit of the hill, which is scattered with the foundations of those early settlers' circular huts.

Newport Castle is part fortress, part manor house – it has been inhabited as a private dwelling for the past 150 years. Built in the 13th century by Norman baron William Fitzmartin, the castle was held for centuries by the powerful lords of Cemaes. As can be seen from its ruined battlements, the fortress was often involved in bloody conflict, first in 1215 when captured and sacked by Llywelyn the Great, Prince of Wales, then by Owain Glyndwr. Fitzmartin also established St Mary's Church, whose impressive Norman square tower vies for dominance with the castle.

The River Nevern divides Newport's two beaches. On the north side there's an excellent sandy beach with safe bathing away from the currents of the river mouth. Parrog beach on the south side is for walkers who can stroll along the clifftops, past thickets of colourful gorse and shimmering sea pinks.

PEMBROKE MAP REF SN0098

Pembroke is an attractive walled town with a 900-year history dating back to its Norman castle, which overlooks the town from its perch on a limestone crag. Surrounded by water on three sides, the castle, built by the Earls of Pembroke, was one of the biggest and most powerful in Wales. The walls of the keep are 7 feet (2m) thick and 75 feet (23m) high. A secret underground passage burrows beneath the Great Hall to the harbour. Harry Tudor, the grandson of John of Gaunt and a descendant of Llywelyn the Great, was born in the castle. On returning from exile he advanced with an army that defeated Richard III at Bosworth Field, after which he was crowned King Henry VII.

In 1977 Pembroke was designated an Outstanding Conservation Area. In the bustling main street, lined with both Georgian and Tudor buildings there are some fascinating shops, cafés and restaurants. If it's peace you're after, a stroll by the river and Mill Pond will take you around the castle walls.

■ Visit

THE GUN TOWER MUSEUM

Built in 1851 to protect the Royal Naval Dockyard at Pembroke, the Gun Tower, which juts out into the wide waterway, now houses a museum illustrating Pembroke's military heritage. You can learn about life as experienced by one of Queen Victoria's soldiers who waited for an invasion that never came, see superb models of the old navy dockyard where more than 200 ships were built, and learn about the World War II flying boats – Pembroke was the world's largest flying boat base.

PRESELI HILLS MAP REF SN1032

The Preseli Hills rise from Cardigan Bay at Fishguard and Newport and reach their highest point at Foel Cwmcerwyn some 1,760 feet (536m) above sea level. They're not that high by Welsh standards but these peaks have always been synonymous with all things spiritual. Preseli has sunsets that light up the whole of Cardigan Bay with a fiery glow, framed by the jagged silhouettes of strangely weathered summit tors.

Buried beneath your feet are the settlers from pre-history: the Neolithic tribes who were here before the 'true Welsh', the Celts, came from across the sea. Cromlechs, the earthwork and stone remains of fortress walls and hut circles are liberally scattered across the map for you to discover. Stonehenge in Wiltshire was built from rocks hewn from the Preselis. The rock that the monoliths were carved from, an igneous spotted dolerite, is exclusive to Carnmenyn on the eastern side of the range.

When the Normans attacked Pembrokeshire they built a line of castles from Pembroke to Roch near St Davids. The Welsh were driven into the foothills of the Preseli and an imaginary line, the Landsker, was to divide the different tongues. If you've first visited the county's English-speaking south coast you may be surprised when you arrive at Rosebush, a tiny village that lies to the south of Foel Cwmcerwyn, for this friendly place is Welsh-speaking. The little village, which is the starting point for the best Preseli walks, has a campsite and one of the best inns in Wales, Tafarn y Sinc.

ST DAVID'S MAP REF SM7525

Set on a windswept plateau, St David's, Britain's smallest city, is as isolated from urban life as it is possible to be. Flanked on either side by jagged dolerite crests of Carn Llidi and Carnedd-lleithr, this looks and feels as if it is an inhospitable corner of the world. And so it was when Dewi, a 6th-century Celtic preacher who was later to become St David, patron saint of Wales, sailed from Ireland to set up his monastery here.

When you arrive in St David's and walk up the High Street past the gift shops, cottages, the boat-trip vendors' offices and the cafés, there are no signs of the grand ecclesiastical buildings. They're hidden in the hollow of the Alun Valley behind Cross Square, and it's only when you descend down the Pebbles to the Bell Tower that they appear. At first glance the cathedral is as austere as the surrounding landscape, yet the purple-hued sandstone and perfect proportions give it an impressive presence. Inside, the cathedral is light and airy, with fine ornamental Norman arches and slightly leaning piers of the nave leading the eye to a splendid roof of Irish oak.

Destroyed several times by the violent Viking raids in pre-Norman days, the oldest part of the current cathedral, the nave, dates back to 1180 – the original tower collapsed in 1220. In the early 14th century Bishop Henry de Gower raised the walls of the aisles, inserted much grander windows and built the south porch, transept chapels and Lady Chapel. A century later Bishop Vaughan built up the tower to its present height and added the splendid roof.

The Reformation left the cathedral neglected and it was damaged during the Civil War. In 1862 George Gilbert Scott was charged with renovating the cathedral. While doing so he discovered two skeletons, believed to be St David and his friend St Justinian, now kept in an oak chest in the Holy Trinity Chapel.

For around nine days in May and June each year, St David's Cathedral holds a festival of classical music. St David's three cathedral choirs attend, as well as many top musicians from around the world.

Across the Alun stream lie the large and magnificent ruins of the Bishop's Palace. The palace was built in the late 12th century, but significantly enlarged by Bishop Henry de Gower between 1328 and 1347 to accommodate the growing number of pilgrims who flocked to St David's each year. St David's became a seat of power, illustrated by the opulent arcaded parapets and the magnificence of the Great Hall. Today the palace is often a venue for concerts and plays. There are two permanent exhibitions: the Lords of the Palace and Life in the Palace of a Prince of the Church.

SAUNDERSFOOT MAP REF SN1305

Once a small fishing village, which flourished with finds of high quality anthracite coal, Saundersfoot has since been caught up in near neighbour Tenby's popularity. It's not hard to see why. Set at the foot of a pleasant wooded valley, the village has an attractive harbour alongside wonderful golden sands. The village is a popular centre for fishing, sailing and water sports.

An Invigorating Trundle Around Strumble

The headland cliffs tower above the pounding Atlantic surf, the path cuts an airy, at times precarious, line across their tops and the sky is alive with the sound of seabirds. Atlantic grey seals, porpoises and even dolphins are regularly spotted in the turbulent waters. Garn Fawr, a formidable rocky tor that lords high above the whole peninsula, brings a touch of hillwalking to the experience, and the shapely lighthouse flashes a constant reminder of just how treacherous these waters can be.

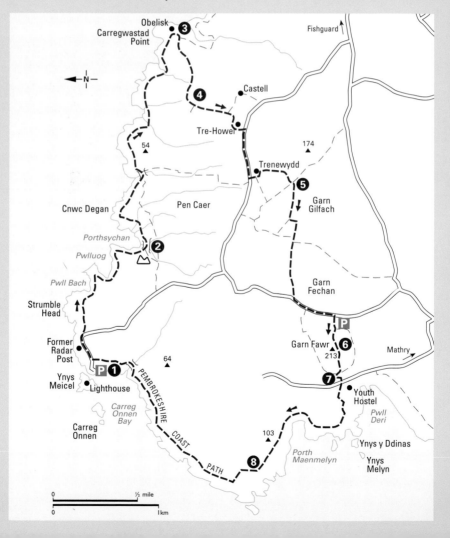

Route Directions

1 Walk back up the road and cross a gate on the left on to the coast path. Pass above the bays of Pwll Bach and Pwlluog, then drop steeply to a footbridge behind the pebble beach of Porthsychan.

2 Follow the coast path waymarkers around Cnwc Degan and down to another bridge, where a couple of footpaths lead away from the coast. Continue along the coast, passing a cottage on the right and climbing and dropping a couple of times, before you reach the obelisk at Carregwastad Point.

3 Follow the main path inland and cross a stile on to a farm track, where you turn right, away from the coast path. Continue with this path, which is vague in places, up through the gorse to a wall, then turn right on to a good track. Take this through a succession of gates and around a left-hand bend.

4 Ignore a track to the right and continue up the cattle track, eventually bearing right into the farmyard where you follow a walkway past livestock pens before swinging left, after the buildings, to the road. Turn right and follow the road past a large house to a waymarked bridleway on the left. Pass Trenewydd and go through a gate on to a green lane. Follow this up to another gate and on to open ground.

5 Turn right here and follow the wall to yet another gate. This leads to a walled track which you follow to the road. Turn left and climb up to the car park beneath Garn Fawr. Turn right, on to a hedged track, and follow this up, through a gap in the wall, and over rocks to the trig point.

6 Climb down and cross the saddle between this tor and the other, slightly lower, one to the south. From here head west towards an even lower outcrop and pass it on the left. This becomes a clear path that leads down to a stile. Cross this and turn left, then right on to a drive that leads to the road.

7 Walk straight across and on to the coast path. Bear right and cross a stile to drop down towards Ynys y Ddinas, the small island ahead. Navigation is easy as you follow the coast path north, over Porth Maenmelyn and up to a cairn.

8 Continue along the coast, towards the lighthouse, until you drop to a footbridge above Carreg Onnen Bay. Cross a stile into a field, then another back on to the coast path and return to the car park.

Route facts

DISTANCE/TIME 8 miles (12.9km) 3h

MAP OS Explorer OL35 North Pembrokeshire

START Car park by Strumble Head, grid ref: SM 894411

TRACKS Coast path, grassy, sometimes muddy tracks, rocky paths, 13 stiles

GETTING TO THE START From Fishguard, minor roads lead northwest to the car park on the very edge of this coastline.

THE PUB The Farmers Arms, Mathry. Tel: 01348 831284; www.farmersarmsmathry. co.uk

❶ Some hillwalking required on Garn Fawr

Island Views from the Marloes Peninsula

The scenic Marloes Peninsula forms the westernmost tip of the southern shores of St Brides Bay. The paddle-shaped headland is a very popular place to walk due to the narrow neck that affords minimum inland walking for maximum time spent on the coast. It is famous for its scenery, which includes two of the Pembrokeshire Coast National Park's finest and least-crowded beaches, some secluded coves that are often inhabited by seals, and some wonderfully rugged coastline. There are also fine views over a narrow but turbulent sound to the small islands of Skomer and Skokholm – two significant seabird breeding grounds. The walking here is captivating, even by Pembrokeshire standards.

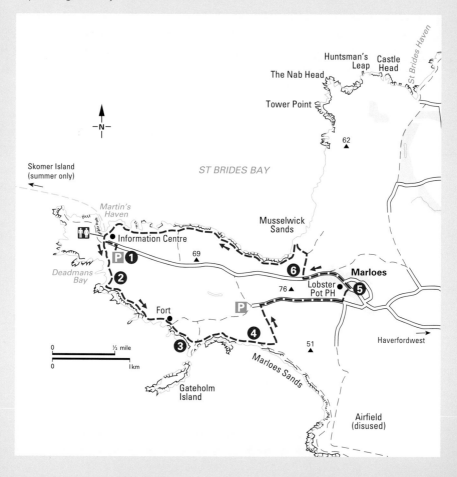

Route Directions

1 From the bottom of the car park, walk down to the bottom of the hill. Bear around to the left, then go through the gate straight ahead into the Deer Park. Turn left and follow the path along to a gate and out on to the coast.

2 With the sea to your right, continue easily along over Deadman's Bay to a stile. The next section cruises along easily, passing the earthworks of an Iron Age fort on the left and crossing another stile as you approach Gateholm Island.

3 It is possible to get across to the island at low tide, but care is needed to scramble over the slippery rocks. To continue the walk, follow the coast path, above the western end of the beautiful Marloes Sands until you drop easily to the main beach access path.

4 Turn left and climb up to the road; turn right here. Follow the road along for around 0.75 mile (1.2km) to a hedged bridleway on the left. Follow this down and turn left into Marloes village.

5 Pass the Lobster Pot on the left and continue ahead to leave the village. Ignore a few tracks on the right, as the road bends around to the left, and continue out into open countryside where you'll meet a footpath on the right.

6 Walk down the edge of the field and bear around to the left to drop back down on to the coast path above Musselwick Sands. Turn left and follow the path west for over 1.5 miles (2.4km) to Martin's Haven. Meet the road and climb past the information centre back to the car park.

Route facts

DISTANCE/TIME 6 miles (9.7km) 2h30

MAP OS Explorer OL36 South Pembrokeshire

START National Trust car park above Martin's Haven, near Marloes village, grid ref: SM 761089

TRACKS Coast path and clear footpaths, short section on tarmac, 9 stiles

GETTING TO THE START Follow the B4327 for approximately 10 miles (16km) southwest of Haverfordwest, then turn right to Marloes. Take the minor road from here to the car park at Martin's Haven

THE PUB St Brides Inn, St Brides. Tel: 01437 781266; www.stbridesinn.co.uk

❶ Slippery rocks on the island

A Tour of Northern Pembrokeshire

From Norman Haverfordwest we cross the Landsker into the land of the Celts and neolithic tribesmen. This tour follows the ancient pilgrims to St David's Cathedral, visits Pembrokeshire's most picturesque coastal village and seeks out one of Britain's largest and best preserved burial chambers at Pentre Ifan before climbing onto the mysterious Preseli Hills, where the blue obelisks of Stonehenge were hewn out of the mountains.

Route Directions

1 From Haverfordwest quayside, head north past Castle Square to reach a roundabout. Take the A487 signed St David's. Across rolling pastureland you'll see Roch Castle perched on a rocky outcrop.

Built by the Normans in the 13th century, Roch Castle is one of the Landsker castles used to repress the Welsh-speaking people and keep them contained in the hills. Nowadays, it offers self-catering holidays.

2 The road descends to the sands at Newgale, where there are quite likely surfers or windsurfers enjoying the waves. After climbing around the headland, the road then descends into the wooded valley sheltering Solva, one of Pembrokeshire's prettiest coastal resorts.

Detour left to see the older lower village and harbour, where there's a good-sized car park. There are plenty of cafés here for morning coffee and a bite to eat, or you could take a short walk over the Gribin to reach the sea cliffs on the headland.

3 Return to the main road, which climbs past the upper village and across more pastures to reach St David's. The pay car park lies at the entrance to the village. The cathedral and the extensive ruins of the Bishop's Palace are unmissable sights.

4 Veer right in the village centre, still following the A487, now signed to Fishguard. After 6 miles (10km), in the hamlet of Croes-goch (the red cross) take the second turning on the left, a minor road passing through Llanrhian where you go straight ahead at the crossroads to return to the coast at Porthgain.

Once a busy port exporting slate and granite around the world, Porthgain's harbour is now the domain of small fishing craft and pleasure boats. If you've worked up an appetite, then stop off at the historic Sloop Inn for lunch – relics and old photos lining the walls give an insight into the history of the village.

5 Return to the A487 and turn left for Fishguard. The road first drops to the coast at Goodwick, from where the coastal A40 road passes the head o the deep-water harbour, before doubling back left at the large roundabout to enter Fishguard. On reaching the bustling town centre stay with the A487 signposted Cardigan, and descend to the more attractive Lower town. You can park here and walk along the quayside, taking in all the water-borne activity of the sea.

6 Beyond Lower Fishguard the A487 climbs away from the harbour and then heads for Newport, a small seaside resort, which is dominated by the ruffle topped Mynydd Carn Ingli.

If a spot of sunbathing would fit the bill, the best beach lies

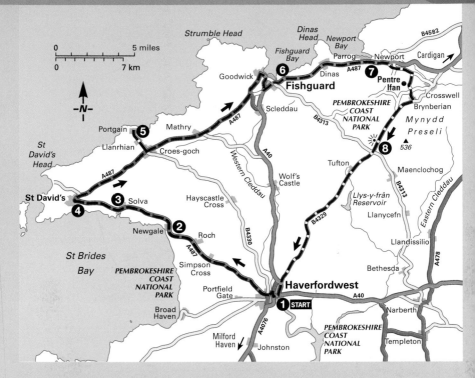

across the Nevern Estuary and is reached using narrow and circuitous lanes. Rather closer at hand is Parrog, where you could stretch your legs along the clifftops. There's also the rather good Morawelon Café Bar if you want more relaxation (turn left on Parrog Road in Newport's centre).

7 Continue along the A487 signed Cardigan, until you see signs for Pentre Ifan on the right. These lead up country lanes to the Iron Age burial cromlech (free). Continue on the lane going straight over at the crossroads to Brynberian. Once through the village turn right on the B4329, which climbs the northern slopes of the Preseli Hills to a high pass (1,330ft/405m) along the main ridge.

It's only a short walk (dry underfoot in summer) up the hill to the right (west), Cerrig Lladron, where there's a view indicator to highlight the superb western panoramas of the Pembrokeshire and Cardigan Bay coastlines.

8 The B road descends all the way back to return to Haverfordwest, but if you're looking for somewhere for supper, turn left at the first crossroads, then left again through the little hamlet of Rosebush to the Tafarn Sinc, a wonderful old-fashioned pub full of characters.

SOLVA MAP REF SM8024

Three miles (5km) east of St David's lies Solva, a village of two parts. The more modern upper village lines the A487 coast road, while in the lower, more attractive part, cottages, small shops and restaurants cluster around the harbour at the sheltered head of a long, winding tidal inlet. These days Solva is a busy little tourist trap but it was founded on maritime traditions. A thriving port until the arrival of the railways, it had several warehouses and a dozen or so limekilns. Solva once boasted a passenger service to New York. However, rather unusually, the passengers would have to bring their own food for a voyage that could last for up to four months!

Though it's a fine place for pottering about and having a spot of lunch, Solva is one of the best bases for a coastal walk, maybe to St David's (get the bus back), or just a stroll along the Gribin, where there's an Iron Age settlement and a perfect view back to the village.

STACKPOLE MAP REF SR9995

The 2,000-acre (810ha) estate, once owned by the powerful Scottish Cawdor family but now managed by the National Trust, is situated between Bosherton, Stackpole and St Govan's Head. It encompasses some of Pembrokeshire's finest coastal scenery.

Bosherton, a tiny village at the western end of the estate, is well situated for a visit to the Bosherton Lily Ponds. These were created by flooding three wooded limestone valleys. It has been claimed that this was the home of the Lady of the Lake and from where

King Arthur gained his magical sword, Excalibur. It's certainly a magical place for nature lovers, who can wander through the surrounding woodland at the waters' edge to reach the seashore at Broad Haven beach. A June visit will reveal water lilies in full splendour, covering the waters of the Western Arm. Visitors include the cormorant, grey heron, kingfisher, coot and moorhen, and you're likely to see one of the many dragonfly, darting across the lakes.

There's another National Trust car park (toll) at Stackpole Quay near to the site of Stackpole Court. The mansion was demolished in 1963 when punitive taxes made it necessary for the Cawdors to dispose of their Welsh assets. The quay, a tiny inlet with a stone-built harbour pier, marks a clearly visible transition between the old red sandstone cliffs of Manorbier and the limestone of southwest Pembrokeshire. A short walk across fields and clifftops leads to some steps descending into Barafundle Bay, a traffic-free golden sandy beach ideal for swimming or a spot of sunbathing. Further sojourns through the pines and sycamores at the far end of the bay take you to the cliffs, arches and stacks of Stackpole Head.

If you time your visit for when the military are not training, you can take the minor road leading south from Bosherton to St Govan's car park. Steps lead down to the 13th-century St Govan's Chapel, a tiny building wedged into a fissure at the base of the cliffs on the site of a Celtic hermit's cell. St Govan, an 11th-century saint, is believed to have been buried beneath the altar.

TENBY MAP REF SN1300

Tenby, by far the biggest and most successful of Pembrokeshire's resorts, is surrounded by caravan sites and it's often buzzing with coach parties and holiday-makers from all backgrounds. On Bank Holidays the town feels like it's going to burst with the weight of its own popularity. But Tenby has undeniable beauty. Brightly colour-washed cottages wrap themselves around a small sandy beach, framed by the pier of the lifeboat station, the harbour and the small boats in the bay. When the coach parties have gone home you can take an after-dinner stroll along the promenade with those cottages and the old castle floodlit against the night sky.

Tenby has two distinct parts. Within the largely intact medieval town walls many of its ancient narrow streets have been cobbled to re-create their authenticity, but outside of these walls, overlooking the large South Beach, the Victorian's influence is there for all to see, with traditional seaside terraces.

Castle Hill looks down on both the old and new towns, but little remained of the castle after its destruction in the Civil War. Much of the town's history from the Stone Age to present times can be traced by visiting the Tenby Museum and Art Gallery on Castle Hill. This includes charters and privileges granted by the Tudors and the Earls of Pembroke.

A devised town trail visits the walls and many of the historic buildings, including the Tudor Merchant's House (National Trust), which is fitted out with authentic furnishings and has three walls with the remains of early frescoes.

■ Activity

RAMSEY ISLAND

You can take the regular Ramsay Island boat from the slipway at St Justinian's, just 3 miles (5km) west of St David's and you will be transported across the fast-flowing Sound and infamous reef known as the Bitches to a haven for wildlife. Ramsay Island's rugged coastline, with its 300-foot (91m) cliffs and isolated rock coves, is home to the largest colony of grey seals in southwest Britain. Two small hills provide exhilarating walks with panoramas of Pembrokeshire's coast and islands through to the distant Preseli Hills.

■ Visit

STACK ROCKS AND THE GREEN BRIDGE OF WALES

Probably the most photographed feature on the Pembrokeshire coastline is the Green Bridge of Wales, a huge natural arch formed by the collapsing of two coastal caverns. It can be viewed from the safe platform on Stack Rocks, which are also known as Elegug Stacks. Before setting out along the road west of the Castlemartin barracks, you'll have to find out if the military are on exercise (Tel: 01646 662367).

■ Activity

CALDEY ISLAND

A boat trip from Tenby to Caldey Island is like a journey back in time, with quiet tracks wending through fields of barley and footpaths seeking out secluded cliff-ringed coves. In 1929 Cistercian monks re-established a monastery on Caldey. They farm the island's 600 acres (240ha) and make perfume from the flowers and herbs. Walkers can seek out the ruins of the old priory or climb to lofty vantage points for stunning views of the coast.

■ TOURIST INFORMATION CENTRES

For general information go to www.visitpembrokeshire.com

Fishguard
Town Hall.
Tel: 01437 776636

Haverfordwest
19 Old Bridge Street.
Tel: 01437 763110

Newport (seasonal)
2 Bank Cottages, Long Street.
Tel: 01239 820912

Pembroke
Commons Road.
Tel: 01646 622388

St David's
Oriel y Parc.
Tel: 01437 720392

Saundersfoot (seasonal)
Harbour Car Park.
Tel: 01834 813672

Tenby
Upper Park Road.
Tel: 01834 842404

■ PLACES OF INTEREST

Caldey Island
Off Tenby. Tel: 01834 844453;
www.caldey-island.co.uk
Take a boat trip from Tenby.
Cistercian monastery, quiet walks, and fine beaches.

Castell Henllys
Off the A487 between Newport (Pembrokeshire) and Cardigan. Tel: 01239 891319;
www.castellhenllys.com

The Gun Tower Museum
Pembroke Dock.
Tel: 01646 622246

Pembrokeshire's naval heritage.

Pembroke Castle
Tel: 01646 684585; www.pembrokecastle.co.uk

St David's Bishop's Palace
St David's, Pembrokeshire.
Tel: 01437 720517
Extensive and impressive ruins next to cathedral. The entry fee includes 'Lords of the Palace' exhibition.

St David's Cathedral
St David's. www.stdavidscathedral.org.uk

Tenby Museum and Art Gallery
Castle Hill, Tenby.
Tel: 01834 842809;
www.tenbymuseum.org.uk

■ FOR CHILDREN

Dinosaur Park
Gumfreston, Tenby.
Tel: 01834 45272;
www.thedinosaurpark.co.uk
A 1-mile (1.6km) long walk complete with prehistoric monsters and woodland trail.

Folly Farm
Begelly, Kilgetty.
Tel: 01834 812731
A family adventure park with a fun fair, theatre, play barn, exotic animals, restaurant and coffee shop.

Oakwood Theme Park
Narberth. Roller coasters and more. Tel: 01834 891376;
www.oakwoodthemepark.co.uk

Teifi Valley Narrow Gauge Railway
Nr Newcastle Emlyn.
Tel: 01559 371077;
www.teifivalleyrailway.coM

■ SHOPPING

Market Days
Fishguard, Thu. Farmers market fortnightly, Sat; Haverfordwest fortnightly, Fri; Pembroke Dock fortnightly, Sat; St David's, Women's Institute market, Thu; Tenby, indoor market, Mon, Tue, Thu–Sat.

■ PERFORMING ARTS

Fishguard
Theatr Gwaun.

Milford Haven
Torch Theatre.

Narberth
Queens Hall.

■ SPORTS & OUTDOOR ACTIVITIES

ANGLING

Boat Fishing
Short trips or day-long deep-sea fishing trips from many harbours.
Tenby: Tel: 07974 623542;
www.tenbyfishing.co.uk
Solva: Tel: 01437 720053;
www.solva.net
Neyland: 01646 600313;
www.celticwildcat.com

Coarse Fishing
Yet-y-Gors Fishery, Manorwen, Fishguard

Tel:01348 873497;
www.yet-y-gors.co.uk
Two coarse lakes plus
still-water fly-fishing
for trout.
Holgan Farm, Narberth.
Tel: 07796 517586;
www.fisheries.co.uk
Carp and tench lakes.

BEACHES

Among the best beaches for
sunbathing and swimming
are those at Barrafundle
(Stackpole), Broadhaven,
Marloes, Saundersfoot,
Tenby, Newport and
Whitesands Bay (St David's).
Always take note of safety
instructions. Watersports
enthusiasts head for
Broadhaven, Freshwater
West, Manorbier and St
Brides Bay.

BOAT TRIPS

Tenby to Caldey Island
Day trips from Tenby Harbour.
Tel: 01834 844453;
www.caldey-island.co.uk
**Neyland/Martin's Haven to
Grassholm, Skokholm and
Skomer**
Tel: 01646 603110;
www.dale-sailing.co.uk
St David's to Ramsey Island
Trips to and around Ramsey,
and wildlife-watching.
www.ramseyisland.co.uk
www.thousandislands.co.uk
www.aquaphobia-
ramseyisland.co.uk
Cardigan Bay

Cetacean watching and trips
from the Teifi Estuary
Tel: 01239 623558 www.
baytoremember.co.uk

CYCLING

Old railways, reservoir roads,
byways, coastal and hill
tracks. For general info visit
www.cyclepembrokeshire.
com
Bike hire
Newport.
Tel: 01239 820773;
www.newportbikehire.com);
Haverfordwest.
Tel: 01437 760068;
www.mikes-bikes.co.uk
Fishguard.
Tel: 01348 874170; www.
pembrokeshirebikes.co.uk
and many other centres.

HORSE RIDING

Dunes Riding Centre
Cotts Lane, Martlewy,
Narberth. Tel: 01834 891398;
www.dunes-riding.co.uk
East Nolton Riding Stables
East Nolton Farm, Nolton
Haven, Haverfordwest.
Tel: 01437 710360;
www.noltonstables.com
Havard Stables
Trewyddig Fawr, Dinas Cross,
Newport. Tel: 01348 811452
Llanwnda Riding & Trekking
Penrhiw Fach, Llanwnda,
Goodwick. Tel: 01348 873595

WALKING

Pembrokeshire Coast Path
National Trail: for information
about walking this long

distance path and hundreds
of other walking routes visit
the National Park website
www.pcnpa.org.uk
Year-round coastal bus
services for walkers (buses
run on chip fat) Tel: 01437
764551 www.pembrokeshire.
gov.uk/coastbus

WATER SPORTS

Coasteering
St David's. Tel: 01437 721611;
www.tyf.com
Kitesurfing
Newgale Beach.
Tel: 07816 169359;
www.bigbluekitesurfing.com
Sea Kayaking
County-wide.
Tel: 01348 837709;
www.preseliadventure.co.uk
Surfing
Newgale, Manorbier,
Freshwater West.
Tel: 01646 680070; www.
outerreefsurfschool.co.uk

■ EVENTS & CUSTOMS

Fishguard
Folk Festival, May
International Music Festival,
June
Jazz festival Sept.
Narberth
Winter carnival, early Dec
Newport/Preseli
Walking Festival, May
St David's
Cathedral festival May/Jun
Tenby
Arts festival late Sept.

Tea Rooms

The Boathouse Tea Room
Stable Yard, Stackpole
SA71 5DE. Tel: 01646 672672
Close to the old stone jetty, this popular licensed café has a large outdoor area for alfresco dining. The quiches are delicious while tasty sandwiches include fresh crab, and cream teas have tempting cakes.

Morawelon Café Bar & Restaurant
Parrog, Newport, Pembrokeshire SA42 0RW
Tel: 01239 820565
Set on the Parrog beachfront, you can indulge yourself here with many varieties of tea or coffee and delicious cakes, or you can tuck into a mouth-watering meal that might include freshly caught local crab, washed down with a cool glass of white wine.

The Old Printing House
20 Main Street, Solva
SA62 6UU. Tel: 01437 721603
The award-winning tea room/ restaurant is located at the heart of the village in an 18th-century house and paper mill with beamed ceilings and stripped stone walls. The tea room is noted for its freshly baked bread and cakes, home-made chutneys and cream teas.

Tudor Lodge Restaurant
Jameston, Manorbier
SA70 7SS. Tel: 01834 871978;
www.tudorlodgerestaurant.
co.uk
This restaurant has a clean, modern style – walls hung with contemporary paintings and a good atmosphere, and traditional, blazing log fires. The food is excellent and prepared using fresh local produce wherever possible, whether it is for light lunches or evening meals.

Pubs

Cambrian Inn
6, Main Street, Solva
SA62 6UU. Tel: 01437 721210;
www.cambrianinn.co.uk
The 16th-century inn sited at the entrance to Lower Solva offers restaurant and bar meals in comfortable cosy surroundings. Expect fresh pasta, steaks and vegetarian dishes with real ales such as Brains Reverend James or Wye Valley Butty Bach.

St Brides Inn
St Brides Road, Little Haven
SA62 3UN. Tel: 01437 781266;
www.stbridesinn.co.uk
This charming little inn has wooden pews inside a compact dining area, with stripped stone walls and an ancient well in one corner. Good food is served here with a daily specials board that often includes locally caught seafood. There's also a beer garden, where meals and barbecues are served throughout the summer.

The Stackpole Inn
Jasons Corner, Stackpole
SA71 5DF
Tel: 01646 672324;
www.stackpoleinn.co.uk
The 17th-century Stackpole Inn is popular with walkers and locals. The award-winning bar and restaurant menu includes fresh locally caught fish that appear on the 'just in' specials board and old favourites such as Welsh black beef.

Tafarn Sinc
Rosebush SA66 7QT
Tel: 01437 532214;
www.tafarnsinc.co.uk
This red-painted corrugated building that used to be a railway halt promises little on first sight, and when you realise that there's sawdust on the floor you might be put off. But this Welsh-speaking, friendly pub has been likened to a museum of local history inside, with old photos and curios on every wall. The pub has its own-brewed beer, Cwrw Tafarn Sinc, and serves delicious food including the most succulent steaks.

Gower Peninsula & Coast

Though not far from the urban valleys of the south, the limestone cliffs and golden sandy bays of the Gower Peninsula have been protected from unsympathetic development – industrial and residential – since it was designated as Britain's first Area of Outstanding Natural Beauty in 1956. Further east, Cardiff is in every sense the capital of Wales. It has a rich industrial, commercial and cultural heritage, but has evolved into a modern, vibrant and cosmopolitan city. Cardiff's docks have become vibrant Cardiff Bay, fringed with restaurants, bars and shops. Among its many attractions are Techniquest, a fantastic science and discovery complex and planetarium and Butetown History and Arts Centre, which traces the area's history – perfect amusement for rainy days. A new Millennium Centre, which opened in 2004, hosts operas, ballet and musicals. You will find that there are not enough hours in a weekend to do Cardiff justice – enjoy its many delights.

10 Walk start point

3 Cycle start point

MEWSLADE BAY

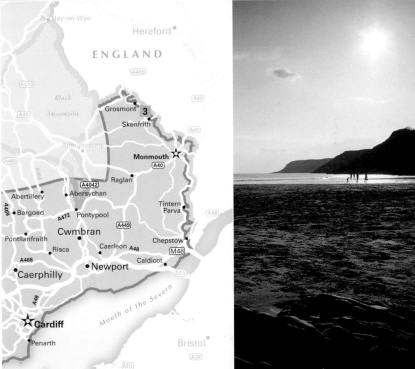

CASWELL BAY

Unmissable attractions

Enjoy shopping, good food, culture and a host of other treats in Cardiff...explore historic Monmouth, the birthplace of Henry V...go in search of Dylan Thomas at Laugharne...explore the Gower Peninsula and discover superb Rhossili Bay and coast...discover two castles at Grosmont and Skenfrith on a quiet cycle ride.

3

1 **Rhossili**
Rhossili Bay is one of the finest stretches of flat sands in Wales.

2 **Cardiff**
Cardiff's Millennium Stadium, in the heart of the city, hosts major sporting events and concerts.

3 **Parkmill**
Remote Three Cliffs Beach takes its name from the three cliffs that project out into the bay. The beach can be accessed via a signed path from Parkmill.

4 **Monmouth**
The narrow, fortified Monmow Bridge and Gatehouse, dating back to the 13th century, crosses the River Monmow at the southwestern edge of Monmouth.

5 **Port Einon Bay**
One of the most popular bays on the Gower, Port Einon is popular with both families and surfers.

4

5

CARDIFF MAP REF ST1876

Today the capital of Wales is the pride of the principality, a flourishing modern city, but one that hasn't forgotten its roots. Its history goes back 2,000 years to the time of the Romans and it's all encompassed within the walls of Cardiff Castle which stands proudly, right in the centre of the city. The moated Norman castle, whose 12th-century keep has survived, was built on the site of the Roman fort – some of the Roman foundation walls can still be seen. Like many Welsh castles, Cardiff was left ruinous by Owain Glyndwr but it was rebuilt by Richard Beauchamp, the Earl of Warwick, and continued to serve as a residence for several centuries.

Cardiff's prosperity, and gradual rise to importance, came with the Industrial Revolution. The discovery of coking coal allowed the iron-smelting industry to flourish in the valleys to the north and Cardiff became the obvious choice as a port. At this time the wealthy Bute family, who were descendants of the royal Stuarts, moved here. They enlarged the docks and made Cardiff into one of the world's largest coal and iron

exporting ports, and they also took possession of Cardiff Castle. The 3rd Marquis of Bute commissioned William Burges to redevelop the living quarters into the Gothic Victorian style you see today. No expense was spared: the interiors were opulent, using marble, gold leaf and fine hardwoods from around the world. Many of the rooms have amazing decorated ceilings, stained-glass windows, murals of historical and mythological figures, and fine works of art on the walls. The ornate clock tower looks over the city, as Big Ben does in London.

The city centre buildings are a mix of modern, Victorian and Edwardian, with shopping arcades criss-crossing the main streets. The classic Portland stone buildings of the Law Courts, City Hall and the National Museum present an impressive front to the Civic Centre and university areas, while the open spaces of Bute Park behind the castle take you to the banks of the River Taff. Here you can catch a waterbus past the famous Cardiff Arms Park and the much larger Millennium Stadium to Cardiff Bay, where the old dockyards, which declined with the end of the Welsh coalfield, have been transformed into a busy, thriving waterfront. The controversial Cardiff Bay Barrage construction has created a massive freshwater lake out of the bay, but still allows the fish to pass through.

On the waterfront the famous terracotta Pierhead Building is joined by two revolutionary buildings: the Senedd Building, which houses the National Assembly of Wales, and the Millennium Centre, which presents the performing

■ Visit

CASTELL COCH – THE RED CASTLE

This fairy-tale castle, a few miles north of Cardiff, echoes those in Bavaria with its circular red sandstone towers and conical roofs. Built on a limestone outcrop on wooded hill-slopes, the original Norman castle had fallen into disrepair, but the 3rd Marquis of Bute commissioned William Burges to refurbish it to the same extravagant standards that he exercised on Cardiff Castle.

arts. The latter built from local slate has a bilingual inscription in large letters: 'In these stones horizons sing', which says a lot about 21st-century Cardiff.

LAUGHARNE & WEST CARMARTHEN COASTLINE
MAP REF SN3010

Lying on the western bank of the Taf, Laugharne, which is pronounced Larn, is dominated by the imposing shell of its Norman castle. The castle is perched on a tree-cloaked cliff looking out across the salt marshes and creeks of the estuary and was immortalised by J M W Turner. The main street, lined with Georgian houses, antiquarian shops and bistros, leads to the unusual whitewashed town hall, which has a modest clock tower. Laugharne and Malmesbury in Wiltshire are the only two United Kingdom towns to have retained a charter granted by Royal Decree. The charter, kept in the town hall, allows the people to be governed by a corporation in addition to other tiers of government.

Laugharne is synonymous with Dylan Thomas, the Welsh poet and author of Under Milk Wood, who lived here off and on for many years. Thomas spent the last four years of his life (1949–53) at the Boathouse. This romantically situated cottage overlooking the estuary is now a museum dedicated to his life and works. Visitors can also view his writing shed, sited on a terrace above the house.

Moving out in Carmarthen Bay the road from Laugharne comes to Pendine, whose firm beach of sands and shells stretches for 7 miles (11km) between Gilman Point to Laugharne Sands. In the

■ Visit

KIDWELLY CASTLE
Built on a steep grassy mound looking down on the River Gwendraeth, Kidwelly is one of the best-preserved castles in South Wales. The old timber castle built by the Normans in the early 12th century was destroyed in a heavy attack by Llywellyn the Great in 1231, but was rebuilt in the 1270s. Unusually, the superb gatehouse forms part of the outer walls. It is now managed by CADW.

early 20th century the beach was considered ideal for world land speed records, including Malcolm Campbell's 146.16mph (235.22kmph) record in 1924. These ended with the fatal accident of Parry Thomas-Jones, whose car, Babs, rolled over in the 1927 attempt for the world land speed record. Babs can be seen in Pendine's Museum of Speed. Note: The beach is owned by the MoD and they do occasionally restrict public access in the area.

MONMOUTH & WYE VALLEY
MAP REF ST5112

Historic Monmouth stands at the confluence of the rivers Wye and Monnow. It was the birthplace of Henry V, whose statue stands in Agincourt Square looking down upon a statue of another of the town's favourite sons, Henry Rolls, aviation pioneer and co-founder of Rolls Royce. Monmouth's 13th-century bridge over the River Monnow is the only one in Britain to have included a fortified Gatehouse, which at one time would have had a portcullis and sentry rampart.

▪ Visit

THE GOWER HERITAGE CENTRE

Themed around a 12th-century water-powered corn mill built by the Norman baron, William de Breos, the Gower Heritage Centre opened in 1990 as a countryside crafts centre. It is open to visitors who can explore the sawmill, wheelwright's shop, miller's cottage, agricultural museum, craft shop and tea room. There's a children's play area and numerous small animals, including chickens and ducks, and recently housed exhibits from the former Maritime Museum in Swansea.

The town is a good base for an exploration of the Wye Valley and its lovely riverside walks. Just a few miles south lies Tintern Abbey, founded by the Cistercian order in the 12th century. Though roofless, the abbey's graceful arches of the Decorated style and great windows remain almost complete, embellished by their exquisite surroundings in the wooded Wye valley.

Chepstow, near the mouth of the Wye, is known for its massive Norman castle, which stands on formidable cliffs high above the river. It's best viewed from the east bank.

PARKMILL MAP REF SS5489

Parkmill shelters in the shady sylvan bowers of Ilston Cwm, a limestone valley that winds its way from inland Gower to the coast at Three Cliff Bay. Centred around the only working mill on the peninsula the village is popular with both tourists who come to see the Gower Heritage Centre, with its craft workshops and museum, and walkers. To the northwest you can take a stroll through the woods of Green Cwm to visit the Giant's Grave, a megalithic tomb dating back to 3500 BC, or head southwards down Ilston Cwm. This route leads through more woodland before continuing beneath the huge dunes of Pennard Burrows, on top of which lie the ruins of Pennard Castle and its neighbouring church. The 13th-century castle, which was built by the Normans, appears in few historical records and has always been dogged by sand encroachment. To this day, known remnants remain buried in the sands for their own preservation.

The now lazy stream meanders and trickles into the beautiful golden sands of Three Cliff Bay beneath the stunning, almost vertical limestone strata of the Three Cliffs. The popular climbers' crags begin a fine stretch of superb cliff scenery past the houses of Southgate to Pwlldu Head. Pwlldu means Blackpool, but that's where the similarity ends, for you'll find yourself looking down from this massive headland to a pebble storm beach at the head of the lovely wooded limestone gorge of the Bishopston Valley.

Surfers love the commercialised Caswell Bay, a sandy cove overlooked by pines and self-catering apartments. At Mumbles the world of Gower has collided with that of urban Swansea. A pier, amusement parlours, ice cream kiosks and cafés make country lovers feel they want to retreat rather quickly back to real Gower, although the children may wish to stay, play and eat.

PORT EINON MAP REF SS4685

After threading through the outskirts of Swansea, the wide-open spaces of Fairwood Common, and flirting with the coast at Pennard, Gower's only major road, the A4118 ends at little Port Einon on the southwest coast. The last stretch through the village is narrow, rarely wide enough for two cars to pass. The village is a mix of Gower's rugged coastline and small-scale commercialism. Dunes and cobbles line a sandy beach, all then surrounded by rugged cliffs dotted with the typical Gower lime-washed cottages. There's a real old-fashioned seaside atmosphere, with beachwear, and bucket and spade shops, a couple of fish and chip shop cafés and a surf shop. However, the visitor is only a short walk away from rugged cliffs and secluded rocky coves. The coast walk to Worms Head and Rhossili is the finest in Gower.

Port Einon gets its name from the 11th-century Welsh prince, Einon ap Owain and it is believed that he built the long-gone Port Einon. The village's history is inextricably linked to the sea. In its heyday of the 19th-century more than 40 oyster skiffs operated from the port, and limestone from a nearby quarry was exported. The blue-green stones you'll see scattered on the shoreline are not part of Gower geology but ballast from the cargo ships.

Tales of smuggling are common and it is said that the old salt house, the ruin beneath the cliffs of the western promontory, was used by the Lucas family as a storehouse for contraband. At one time there were eight customs and excise officers based here. Next to the salt house is the youth hostel. The building was formerly a lifeboat station but this was closed following a rescue attempt that went dreadfully wrong. Called out during a winter storm of 1916 the volunteer crew were caught out by horrendous waves, which capsized the boat twice, drowning three of the crew. A monument has been erected in the churchyard as a tribute to their bravery.

Oxwich Point separates Port Einon Bay from the larger sandy sweep of Oxwich Bay, an ideal location for swimming and surfing and also appealing to nature lovers who can visit the nature reserve. The ruins of Sir Rice Mansel's magnificent Tudor mansion, known as Oxwich Castle are perched on the headland overlooking the bay. It is now managed by CADW.

◼ Visit

OXWICH NATIONAL NATURE RESERVE

As an area of Outstanding Natural Beauty, Oxwich Bay combines wildlife with all the appeal of a superb beach resort. It is an excellent location for swimming, surfing and nature appreciation. The beach is easily accessible and the reserve supports several diverse wildlife habitats, including freshwater lakes and marshes, swamps, salt marshes, dunes, cliffs and woodland. The freshwater marsh was artificially created when Sir Thomas Mansel Talbot of Penrice Estate built a wall to prevent encroachment from the sea. The reserve has more than 600 species of flowering plants. You are likely to see ringed plovers, curlews, oystercatchers and gulls feeding on the wet sands at low tide, along with wigeons and warblers on the marshes.

A Trail of Two Castles – Skenfrith and Grosmont

This cycle tour passes through a sleepy corner of Monmouthshire, a lovely part of the country where rolling verdant hills rise from crystal streams and quiet country lanes are lined with flower-decked grass verges. You'll discover two forgotten fortresses, and attractive country pubs and cafés which are conveniently dotted along the route offering a chance to stop for a drink or a bite to eat.

Route Directions

1 Skenfrith is a delightful place in summer. The low-lying castle ruins include a keep surrounded by a four-towered curtain wall. Beautifully sited between the village green and the banks of the Monnow, sunny summer days see the castle surrounded by picnickers, many eating ice creams from the shop opposite. Leave Skenfrith on the narrow northbound lane, passing St Brigit's church, where the road winds past the last of the cottages. The very narrow road lined by hedgerow wends it way through streamside farm pastures, before coming to a T-junction with the B4347.

2 Turn left here, then right at the next junction along the B4521 signed Abergavenny. Beyond the scattered hamlet

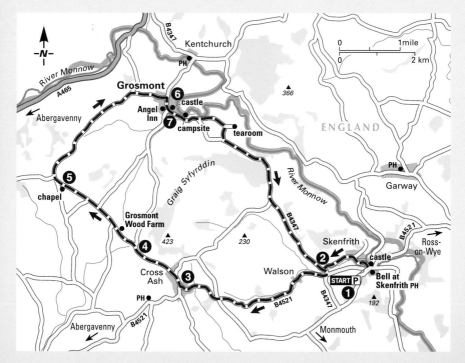

of Walson the road climbs steadily uphill. Stay with the B-road at the next crossroads, ignoring the right turn to 'Dawn of the Day'. Beyond this there's a winding downhill section into the hamlet of Cross Ash.

3 At Cross Ash leave the B-road by a bus shelter on a sharp left-hand bend and turn right for Grosmont. Take the wider left fork at the next junction, heading steadily uphill with the partially wooded hill of Graig Syfyrddin up on the right.

4 Take the left fork, descending past Grosmont Wood Farm. Views have opened out to show first the distinctive craggy outlines of Ysgyryd Fawr (the Skirrid), then sweeping panoramas of the long ridges of the Black Mountains paraded across the fields of the Monnow Valley. A lane joins in from the left, then you keep straight ahead at the next junction.

5 The road passes an old chapel and a cluster of houses at the junction with the Llanfihangel Crucorney road. Turn right here by the phone kiosk and continue now following the undulating lane signed for Grosmont. After 2.5 miles (4km) turn right

along a narrow lane, again signed to Grosmont, to descend into the village.

6 Turn right long the B4347 through the attractive award-winning village, whose cottages have lovely gardens. The whitewashed Angel Inn, which is set back from an unusual sandstone village hall, offers a choice of tasty bar meals and West Country ales and has a pleasant beer garden to the rear. Gentle Jane's Tearoom is just down the road near the spired church. The castle, which is off to the left at the end of a short narrow lane overlooking the River Monnow, is surrounded by a deep moat – dry these days – and the skeletons of its ruined curtain walls, three towers and a gatehouse look rather gaunt against their verdant backdrop. The 14th-century squire, Henry of Grosmont, Duke of Lancaster, had the castle modified to provide luxurious living quarters.

7 Returning to the B-road, continue downhill past the campsite, ignoring the minor right fork lane. The route has now entered the picturesque Monnow Valley. The river meanders wildly, sheltered by green rolling hills and broad-leaved copses. If you didn't eat

Route facts

DISTANCE/TIME 13.5 miles (22km) 3h30

MAP OS Explorer OL13/14; OS Landranger Sheet 161

START Skenfrith Castle, Nr Monmouth, grid ref: SO 457202

TRACKS Quiet B-road and country lanes

GETTING TO THE START Skenfrith lies 8 miles (13km) northeast of Monmouth. Take the A466 out of Monmouth then turn left on the B4521 signed Skenfrith. Turn right by the Bell at Skenfrith pub and park on the right by the castle (free).

THE PUB The Angel Inn, Grosmont. Tel: 01981 240646

CYCLE HIRE Pedalabikeaway, Hadnock Road, Monmouth NP25 3NG Tel: 01600 772821; www.pedalabikeaway.co.uk

at Grosmont, the Part y Seal tea room is a well-signposted short detour on the left. Beyond the tea room the lane climbs right on the north side of Graig Syfyrddin. Ignore the minor right fork beyond its woodland cloak and leave the Monnow Valley behind. The road meets the outward route at point 2, where you turn left and continue on the narrow lane back to the start at Skenfrith.

Through Woodland to Oxwich Point

Once a busy port that paid its way by shipping local limestone from the quarries on the rugged headland, Oxwich is now one of the prettiest and most unspoilt of the Gower villages, due in no small part to its distance from the main roads. The walk can be combined with a visit to Oxwich National Nature Reserve, a treasure trove of marshland and sand dunes in a superb beachside location. The wonderful coastal scenery includes the beautiful and usually deserted beach known as The Sands. And finally, as it is short, the walk allows plenty of time for exploring the atmospheric St Illtud's Church, which was founded in the 6th century, and wandering among the majestic ruins of Oxwich Castle.

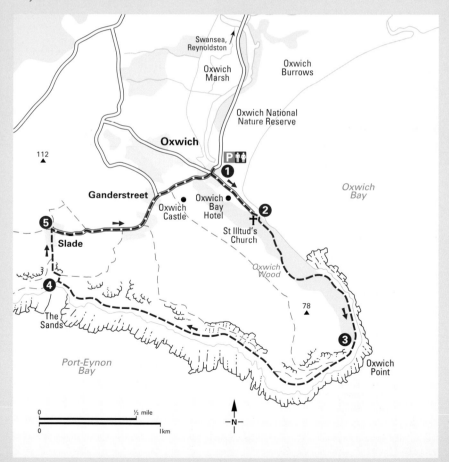

Route Directions

1 Walk back out of the car park and turn left to a crossroads. Turn left here (waymarked 'Eglwys') and pass the Woodside Guesthouse and the Oxwich Bay Hotel, on your right. This lane leads into the woods and up to 6th-century St Illtud's Church, where a gate marks the end of the road and the start of a path leading out on to Oxwich Point.

2 Join the path that runs beneath the church, and follow it for a few paces before going up wooden steps that climb steeply into the wood. As the footpath levels, bear left to drop back down through the wood and around the headland until it comes out into the open above Oxwich Point.

3 The path drops through gorse and bracken to become a grassy coast path that runs easily above a rocky beach. Keep the sea on your left and ignore any tracks that run off to the right. After approximately 1 mile (1.6km) you'll pass a distinct valley that drops in from your right. Continue past this and you'll be funelled into a narrow,

fenced section with a field to your right. Cross a succession of stiles, and you'll eventually reach a path diversion that points you right, away from the beach.

4 Follow this to a stile and a broad farm track, where you turn left. Continue up and around to the right until you come to a galvanised kissing gate. Go through this and keep right to head up a lane past some houses and to a crossroads.

5 Turn right here and follow the road along to a fork where you keep right. Drop down to the entrance of Oxwich Castle on the right. After looking at or exploring the castle, turn right, back on to the lane, and head down into Oxwich village. Keep straight ahead to the car park.

Route facts

DISTANCE/TIME 4.5 miles (7.2km) 2h

MAP OS Explorer 164 Gower

START Oxwich Bay, grid ref: SS 500864

TRACKS Clear paths through woodland, along coast and across farmland, quiet lane, 4 stiles

GETTING TO THE START The village of Oxwich is reached by taking the A4118 west from Swansea. Beyond Nicholaston, take a minor road on the left to travel south for just over a mile into the village. The car park is on your left.

THE PUB King Arthur Hotel, Reynoldston.
Tel: 01792 390775;
www.kingarthurhotel.co.uk

RHOSSILI MAP REF SS4188

At the western end of the peninsula facing Carmarthen Bay, Rhossili is the pride of Gower: a perfect, gently arcing sandy beach flanked by the 250-foot (76m) sandstone cliffs and steep grassy flanks of Rhossili Down. Each day high tide makes islands out of the tiny outcrop of Burry Holms in the north and the one-mile long rocky spit of Worms Head in the south. On many days the breeze is up and the bay is full of surfers riding the waves. When the tide is out you'll see the wooden skeleton of the coaster, Helvetia, driven ashore by the gales of 1887. Rhossili Down at 632 feet (193m) is the highest place on Gower; there's a splendid bridleway straddling its heights. On the summit are the Sweyne's Howes burial chambers.

Rhossili village has one large hotel and a National Trust information centre and shop. A large car park gives access to the long beach and to Worms Head. Tides are of the utmost importance for those wanting to scramble across the rocky causeway to the headland: consult the timetables posted on the National Trust shop and the coastguard's station.

SWANSEA MAP REF SS6593

Little is recorded of Swansea until the Norman conquerors saw its potential as a port. In 1106 Henry de Beaumont, 1st earl of Warwick, built a motte and bailey castle on a cliff overlooking the mouth of the Tawe. After the Welsh sacked the castle in the 13th century, the old structure was rebuilt. The current building dates back to the 14th century, though it didn't have much of a strategic role following the defeat of the Welsh by Edward I. In 1306 Swansea was given the Royal Charter to build and repair ships, a tradition continued into the 20th century.

During the 19th century large-scale anthracite mining and the metal industry changed this small village into the metropolis it is today. By the 1850s the railways had arrived, the first dockyard had been completed and Swansea was supplying 60 per cent of the world's copper requirements. Swansea's other face was of that of a seaside resort – railway adverts compared Swansea Bay with the Bay of Naples and well-to-do Victorians came to take the sea air.

World War II bombing and the mid-20th-century decline in manufacturing saw the city having to re-invent itself. Still a little down-at-heel in the suburbs, Swansea has become a vibrant city, full of culture and new ideas. The dock area has been redeveloped into an opulent Maritime Quarter, where refurbished old buildings share streets with modern architecture such as the National Waterfront Museum, and where you can see vivid reminders of the city's industrial and maritime past. Take a stroll around the 600-berth yachting marina and over the elegant Sail Bridge across the Tawe, then pop in to see the exhibition at the Dylan Thomas Centre.

A fine shopping centre surrounds the castle. Music lovers can see international artists at Brangwyn Hall or operas at the Grand Theatre. The Glynn Vivian Art Gallery, which has a fine collection of paintings and sculpture from old masters and modern artists, also has displays of Swansea porcelain.

■ TOURIST INFORMATION CENTRES

Caerleon
5 High Street.
Tel: 01633 422656

Cardiff Visitor Centre
The Old Library, The Hayes.
Tel: 02920 873573;
www.visitcardiff.com

Chepstow
Castle Car Park, Bridge
Street. Tel: 01291 623772

Mumbles
522 Mumbles Road.
Tel: 01792 361302

Monmouth
Priory Street.
Tel: 01600 713899;
www.visitwyevalley.com

Swansea
Plymouth Street.
Tel: 01792 468321;
www.visitswanseabay.com

■ PLACES OF INTEREST

The Big Pit:
National Coal Museum
Blaenavon.
Tel: 01496 790311;
www.museumwales.ac.uk
Free.

The Boat House
Dylan's Walk, Laugharne
Tel: 01994 427420; www.
dylanthomasboathouse.com

Caerleon
www.caerleon.net
Roman fort. Free.

Caerphilly Castle
Tel: 029 2088 3143;
www.caerphillycastle.com

Cardiff Castle
Tel: 029 2087 8100;
www.cardiffcastle.com

Castell Coch
Tel: 02920 810101

Dylan Thomas Centre
Somerset Place, Swansea.
Tel: 01792 463980

Gower Heritage Centre
Parkmill, Gower.
Tel: 01792 371206; www.
gowerheritagecentre.co.uk

Llandaff Cathedral
Free.

Llanerch Vineyard
Hensol, Pendoylan, Vale of
Glamorgan.
Tel: 01443 225877;
www. llanerch-vineyard.co.uk
Free.

Museum of Speed
Pendine. Tel: 01994 453488
Interpretation of the use of
the sands at Pendine for land
speed attempts and racing.
Free.

The National Botanic Garden
of Wales
Llanarthne.
Tel: 01558 668768;
www.gardenofwales.org.uk

National Museum
Cathays Park, Cardiff.
Tel: 029 20397951; www.
museumwales.ac.uk Free.

National Waterfront Museum
Oystermouth Road, Swansea.
Tel: 01792 638950;
www.museumwales.ac.uk
Tells the story of the
industrialisation of Wales

with exhibits, including
working engines. Free.

National Wetland
Centre Wales
Burry Inlet, Llanelli.
Tel: 01554 7410877;
www.wwt.org.uk/llanelli

Raglan Castle
Tel: 01291 690228
Off A40 between Monmouth
and Abergavenny.

Rhondda Heritage Park
Lewis Merthyr Colliery,
Trehafod.
 Tel: 01443 682036;
www.rhonddaheritagepark.
com

Tintern Abbey
Wye Valley.
Tel: 01291 689251

■ FOR CHILDREN

Pembrey Country Park
Burry Port.
Tel: 01554 833913 (Parks
Manager). Seaside park with
crazy golf, dry ski slope,
toboggan run and a miniature
railway.

■ PERFORMING ARTS

Blake Theatre
Monmouth. Tel: 01600 719401

Brangwyn Hall
Swansea. Tel: 01792 635432

Chapter Arts Centre
Cardiff. Tel: 029 2031 1050

Grand Theatre
Swansea. Tel: 01792 475715

Millennium Centre
Cardiff. Tel: 02920 636464

St David's Hall
Cardiff. Tel: 029 2087 8444
Savoy Theatre
Monmouth. Tel: 01600 772467

■ SPORTS & OUTDOOR ACTIVITIES
BEACHES
Barry Island
Two excellent beaches for bathers.
Carmarthenshire
Cefn Sidan, Pembrey Sands. Eight miles (13km) of fine sands and dunes accessed from Pembrey Country Park near Burry Port. Patrolled by lifeguards in summer.
Caswell Bay
Excellent small beach, popular with surfers. Good café. No dogs May–Sep.
Glamorgan Heritage Coast
Porthcawl.
The town's four beaches here are popular for bathing and watersports.
Oxwich Bay
Sand dunes overlook Gower's second largest beach. Good for bathing, canoeing and sailing, also surfing when the wind is up.
Pendine Sands
An 'endless' beach that once facilitated land speed record attempts.
Port Einon Bay
Commercialised beach with cafés, campsites and gift shops. No dogs May–Sep.

Rhossili Bay
Huge crescent-shaped sandy cove, popular with surfers and hang-gliders.
BOAT TRIPS
Gower Coast
Speedboat trips in a rigid inflatable.
Tel: 07866 250440; www.gowercoastadventures.co.uk
Bay Island Voyages
Lock Keeper's Cottage, Britannia Park Cardiff. Cruises around Cardiff Bay and the coast.
Tel: 01446 420692; www.bayisland.co.uk
CYCLING
Sustrans-approved trails include:
Cardiff: Taff Trail to Brecon Beacons
Llanelli: Swiss Valley & Millennium Coastal Park
Monmouth: Peregrine Path
CYCLE HIRE
Abergavenny
Pedalaway Tel: 01873 830219
www.pedalaway.co.uk
Cardiff Bay
Pedal Power
Tel: 07775 616411; www.cardiffpedalpower.org
Llanelli
Merlin Cycle Tours
Tel: 01554 756603; www.merlincycletours.co.uk
Monmouth
Pedalabikeaway
Tel: 01600 772821; www.pedalabikeaway.co.uk

HORSE RIDING
Llanthony Riding and Trekking
Court Farm, Llanthony.
Tel: 01873 890359; www.llanthony.co.uk
Marros Riding Centre
Marros, Pendine.
Tel: 01994 453238; www.marros-farm.co.uk
Parc-Le-Breos Riding Centre
Penmaen, Gower.
Tel: 01792 371636; www.parc-le-breos.co.uk
SURFING
Rhossili
Sam's Surf Shack
Rhossili, Gower SA3 1PL
Tel: 01792 390519; www.samssurfshack.com

■ EVENTS & CUSTOMS
Cardiff
Cardiff Summer Festival, Jul–Aug.
Chepstow
Agricultural Show, mid-Aug.
Crickhowell
Crickhowell Walking Festival, Mar. Tel: 01873 811970; www.crickhowellfestival.com
Gower
Gower Walking Festival, mid-Jun. Tel: 01792 361302; www.visitmumbles.co.uk
Monmouth
Monmouth Show, end Aug.
Swansea
Swansea Festival of Music and Arts. Celebration of arts and entertainment, Oct.

Tea Rooms

The Bay Bistro & Coffee House

Rhossili, Gower SA3 1PL
Tel: 01792 390519
Enjoy magnificent views across the bay while enjoying hot chocolate, a laverbread burger or a baked Camembert; great cream teas and cakes too! Evening meals include the freshest local fish.

Norwegian Church

Harbour Drive, Cardiff Bay, Cardiff CF10 4PA
Tel: 02920 877959
Built in 1869 as a place of worship for the large number of Scandinavian sailors in Cardiff, the white wooden building has a popular tea room where you can indulge yourself with excellent cakes and a range of snacks.

Part y Seal

Grosmont, Monmouthshire NP7 8LE. Tel: 01981 240814
Here you can enjoy a relaxing morning coffee, lunch or afternoon tea in a splendid rural setting. The old stone cottage has delightful gardens for alfresco summer dining or glowing fires for the short winter days. The produce is home grown and organic. There's also an Oriental giftware shop and

Fairytaleland with its seasonally changing scenes.

Café at the National Waterfront Museum

Oystermouth Road, Maritime Quarter, Swansea SA1 3RD
Tel: 01792 638950
At the heart of the ultra-modern museum buildings in Swansea's Maritime Quarter, the café offers a good choice of excellent cakes, sandwiches, quiches, various savouries and appetising hot meals. Everything is made on-site using fresh produce which is sourced locally wherever possible.

Pubs

Abbey Hotel

Llanthony Priory, Llanthony, Monmouthshire NP7 7NN
Tel: 01873 890487
Many pubs are next door to a church, but this one is in the grounds of the Cistercian priory. Serves lunches and evening meals (also ice creams and hot drinks). Refreshments under the cloisters – what a setting!

Bell at Skenfrith

Skenfrith, Monmouthshire NP7 8UH. Tel: 01600 750235
Splendidly sited by the bridge at Skenfrith, this luxurious 17th-century coaching inn serves fine cuisine sourced

'from as many local farms and suppliers as possible'. Main courses might include fillet of Brecon beef or glazed breast of local duck. The food is complemented by a good wine list and real ales, including Wye Valley and Kingstone, and Ty Gwyn local scrumpy cider.

Castle View Hotel

Bridge Street, Chepstow NP16 5EZ. Tel: 01291 620349; www.hotelchepstow.co.uk
A 300-year-old, ivy-clad, whitewashed pub looking across to the castle and the River Wye. Superb cuisine showcases British specialities with local produce including steaks, and salmon caught from the Wye. There's a charming small beer garden.

King Arthur Hotel

Higher Green, Reynoldston, Gower SA3 1AD
Tel: 01792 390775; www.kingarthurhotel.co.uk
Set back from the large village green, the King Arthur Hotel is well-known for its local Welsh dishes including game steaks, pork, laverbread and locally caught fish and cockles. There's a cosy atmosphere with log fires and for summer there's a pleasant garden.

■ USEFUL NUMBERS

Brecon Beacons National Park Visitors/Mountain Centre
Libanus, Brecon, Powys
Tel: 01874 623366
The Gower Society
Swansea Museum, Victoria Road, Swansea. www.gower society.welshnet.co.uk
Pembrokeshire Coast National Park Centre
Oriel y Parc, St David's.
Tel: 01437 720392;
www.orielyparc.co.uk
Snowdonia National Park Authority
Penrhyndeudraeth, Gwynedd
Tel: 01766 770274;
www.eryri-npa.gov.uk
Visit Wales Centre
Tel: 08708 300 306;
www.visitwales.co.uk

■ ANCIENT MONUMENTS

Most castles, abbeys and ruins in Wales are managed by CADW
Cadw
Plas Carew,
Unit 5/7 Cefn Coed,
Parc Nantgarw,
Cardiff CF15 7QQ
Tel: 01443 336000;
www.cadw.wales.gov.uk

■ ANGLING

Visit Wales publish a free brochure with a list of tackle shops and places to fish, available from TICs or from www.fishing.visitwales.com

■ CYCLING

Visit Wales publish a free brochure, available from TICs or their website www.cycling.visitwales.com
A National cycle network, including a trans-Wales route from Chepstow to Holyhead, Lon Las Cymru, is operated by Sustrans National Cycle Network. Tel: 0117 926 8893; www.sustrans.org.uk

■ WALKING

Visit Wales
www.walking.visitwales.com
NATIONAL LONG DISTANCE PATHS
The Cambrian Way
A 275-mile (444km) route over the Brecon Beacons, Mid Wales and Snowdonia.
Offa's Dyke Path
A 170-mile (274km) route from Chepstow to Prestatyn.
Glyndwr's Way
A 132-mile (212km) route through Mid-Wales.
Pembrokeshire Coast Path
A 186-mile coastal route from Tenby to St Dogmaels.

■ VISITORS WITH DISABILITIES

Disabilities Wales
Tel: 029 20887325;
www.disabilitywales.org

■ ORDNANCE SURVEY MAPS

ANGLESEY & LLEYN PENINSULA
OS Landranger 1:50,000:
Sheets 114, 115, 123, 124
OS Explorer 1:25,000:
Sheets 253/4, 262/3
SNOWDONIA
OS Landranger 1:50,000:
Sheets 115, 125, 126, 137, 148
OS Explorer 1:25,000:
Sheets OL17, OL18, OL23
NORTHEAST WALES & MARCHES
OS Landranger 1:50,000:
Sheets: 116, 124, 125, 135
OS Explorer 1:25,000:
Sheets 214-216, 239, 240, 264/5, 255/6
BRECON BEACONS & MID WALES
OS Landranger 1:50,000:
Sheets 135/6, 146/7, 160/1
OS Explorer 1:25,000:
Sheets OL12/3, 186-188, 198-200, 213-215
PEMBROKESHIRE
OS Landranger 1:50,000:
Sheets 145, 157,158
OS Explorer 1:25,000:
Sheets OL35, 36, 176, 177
GOWER PENINSULA & COAST
OS Landranger 1:50,000:
Sheets 159, 161/2, 170/1
OS Explorer 1:25,000
Sheets 177/8, 164/5, 151/2, OL14

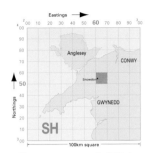

The National Grid system covers Great Britain with an imaginary network of grid squares. Each is 100km square in area and is given a unique alphabetic reference, as shown in the diagram above.

These squares are sub-divided into one hundred 10km squares, identified by vertical lines (eastings) and horizontal lines (northings). The reference for the square a feature is located within is made by adding the numbers of the two lines which cross the bottom left corner of that square to the alphabetic reference (ignoring the small figures). The easting is quoted first. For example, SH6050.

For a 2-figure reference, the zeros are omitted, giving just SH65. In this book, we use 4-figure references, which allow us to pinpoint the feature more accurately by dividing the 10km square into one hundred 1km squares. These squares are not actually printed on the road atlas but are estimated by eye. The same process is carried out as before, giving an enhanced reference of SH6154.

Key to Atlas

M4	Motorway with number	
S Fleet	Motorway service area	
	Motorway toll	
11	Motorway junction with and without number	
3	Restricted motorway junctions	
	Motorway and junction under construction	
A3	Primary route single/dual carriageway	
BATH	Primary route destinations	
	Roundabout	
Y 5 Y	Distance in miles between symbols	
A1123	Other A Road single/dual carriageway	
B2070	B road single/dual carriageway	
	Unclassified road single/dual carriageway	
	Road tunnel	

Toll	Toll	
	Road underconstruction	
	Narrow Primary route with passing places	
→	Steep gradient	
—○—×—	Railway station and level crossing	
+++++++	Tourist railway	
– – – –	National trail	
....	Forest drive	
	Heritage coast	
	Ferry route	
6	Walk start point	
1	Cycle start point	
3	Tour start point	

⛪	Abbey, cathedral or priory	
🐠	Aquarium	
⚔	Castle	
⌒	Cave	
	Country park	
	County cricket ground	
	Farm or animal centre	
✿	Garden	
	Golf course	
	Historic house	
	Horse racing	
	Motor racing	
🏛	Museum	
⊕	Airport	
Ⓗ	Heliport	
	Windmill	
NT	National Trust property	

NTS	National Trust for Scotland property	
	Nature reserve	
★	Other place of interest	
P·R	Park and Ride location	
	Picnic site	
	Steam centre	
	Ski slope natural	
	Ski slope artificial	
i	Tourist Information Centre	
	Viewpoint	
V	Visitor or heritage centre	
	Zoological or wildlife collection	
	Forest Park	
	National Park (England & Wales)	
	National Scenic Area (Scotland)	

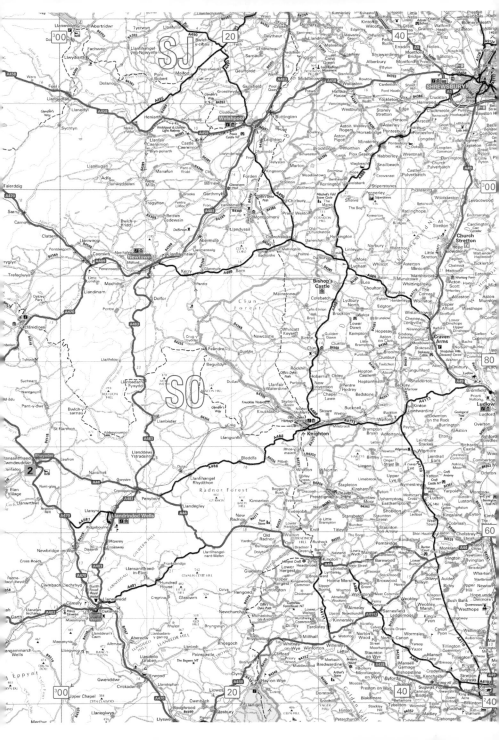

The Automobile Association would like to thank the following photographers and companies for their assistance in the preparation of this book. Abbreviations for the picture credits are as follows – (t) top; (b) bottom; (c) centre; (l) left; (r) right; (AA) AA World Travel Library

1 AA; 4/5 AA/H Williams; 8t AA/C Jones; 8cl AA/P Aithie; 8bl AA/S Watkins; 8r AA/N Jenkins; 9 AA/Stephen Lewis; 10t AA/G Munday; 10c AA/C Jones; 10b AA/I Burgum; 11t AA/N Jenkins; 11b Cardiff Tourist Board; 13t AA/H Williams; 13b AA/N Jenkins; 14 AA/N Jenkins; 18 AA/G Munday; 21t AA/I Burgum; 21b AA/G Matthews; 22 AA/G Munday; 23t AA/G Munday; 23c AA/I Burgum; 23b AA/P Aithie; 25 AA/H Williams; 34 AA/G Munday; 37 AA/C Jones; 39tl AA/M Allwood-Coppin; 39tr AA/S Watkins; 39b AA/M Bauer; 40c AA/S Watkins; 40bl AA/N Jenkins; 40br AA/D Croucher; 41t AA/M Bauer; 41c AA/C Jones; 41b AA/C Jones; 49 AA/S Watkins; 57 AA/S Lewis; 64 AA/G Matthews; 66 AA/N Jenkins; 69t AA/I Burgum; 69b AA/I Burgum; 70cl AA/R Newton; 70cr AA/N Jenkins; 70b AA/C & A Molyneaux; 71t AA/G Munday; 71b AA/D Croucher; 76 AA/C Jones; 84 AA/C & A Molyneaux; 86 AA/M Adelman; 89 AA/C & A Molyneaux; 90cl AA/D Santillo; 90cr AA/C Molyneaux; 90b AA/D Santillo; 91t AA/R Eames; 91b AA/M Adelman; 104 AA/N Jenkins; 106 AA/M Moody; 109t AA/C Warren; 109b AA/N Jenkins; 110cl AA/M Allwood-Coppin; 110cr AA/M Moody; 110b AA/C Molyneaux; 111t AA/C Warren; 111b AA/I Burgum; 126 AA/R Ireland; 128 AA/Mari Sterling; 131t AA/I Burgum; 131b AA/H Williams; 132c AA/M Moody; 132b AA/N Jenkins; 133t AA/N Jenkins; 133c AA/I Burgum; 133b AA/I Burgum; 143 AA; 146 AA/C Jones.

Every effort has been made to trace the copyright holders, and we apologise in advance for any accidental errors. We would be happy to apply the corrections in the following edition of this publication.

LINDENHURST MEMORIAL LIBRARY

DISCARD

4/11

LINDENHURST MEMORIAL LIBRARY
LINDENHURST, NEW YORK 11757